Finding God in Unexpected Places

# Finding
# God
# in
# Unexpected
# Places

## Philip Yancey

WATERBROOK
PRESS

FINDING GOD IN UNEXPECTED PLACES
PUBLISHED BY WATERBROOK PRESS
12265 Oracle Blvd., Suite 200
Colorado Springs, Colorado 80921
*A division of Random House, Inc.*

All Scripture quotations, unless otherwise indicated, are taken from the *Holy Bible, New International Version*®. NIV®. Copyright © 1973, 1978, 1984 by International Bible Society. Used by permission of Zondervan Publishing House. All rights reserved.

ISBN 1-57856-961-3

This book is copublished with Doubleday, a division of Random House, Inc.

Original edition first published in 1995 in the United States by Moorings, a division of the Ballantine Publishing Group, Random House, Inc., New York. Subsequently published in 1997 by Vine Books, an imprint of Servant Publications. Some of the material in this book was previously published in different forms in the following periodicals: *Christianity Today, Marriage Partnership,* and *World Vision.*

Library of Congress Cataloging-in-Publication Data
Yancey, Philip.
    Finding God in unexpected places / Philip Yancey.—[New ed.].
        p.   cm.
    Includes bibliographical references.
    ISBN 0-385-51309-7 (alk. paper)
    1. Christian life—Meditations.   2. God—Omnipresence—Meditations.
3. Yancey, Philip.   I. Title.

    BV4501.3.Y35 2005
    242—dc22              2004056172

Printed in the United States of America
2005

10  9  8  7  6  5  4  3  2

# Contents

✠

## Part Three: Finding God in the Rubble

## Part Four: Finding God in a Fractured Society

## Part Five: Finding God Among the Headlines

## Part Six: Finding God in the Cracks

## Part Seven: Finding God Within the Church

# Introduction

†

I began my career back in 1971 as a magazine journalist. Every month I would write four or five articles on a wide variety of topics. I liked the quick pace, the vicarious thrill of leeching other lives more exciting than mine, and the sense of guilt-free writing (magazines usually get thrown away, so if I wrote something boring or stupid one month, I could try to improve on it the next).

The process of writing books required some adjustments. I had to be more careful because a book can stay in print a long time. If I made a factual error or took a controversial position, I might still be hearing about it a decade later.

I also had to learn to adjust my attention span. I read somewhere that in the early days of the Alaska Highway, tractor-trailer trucks would make deep ruts in the gravel as they carried construction equipment to boomtowns up north. Someone posted this sign at the beginning of the road: CHOOSE YOUR RUT CARE-

FULLY, YOU'LL BE IN IT FOR THE NEXT 200 MILES. It takes me between one and two years to write a book, and if I don't choose carefully, that time period may well seem like an endless rut.

Perhaps because I've never outgrown the journalism instinct, I intersperse my book projects with travel and articles. For twenty years I have written a column on the back page of *Christianity Today* magazine, and I've made it a habit not to think about that column until the deadline day arrives. For one day a month, at least, I can keep a little spontaneity in my writing life. The next day, I rejoin the rut.

This book is a bit of a hybrid because in it I have pulled together spontaneous pieces, added others, and reworked them into something that I hope takes shape as a book. I can look back over the past years' work and see the topics and trends that have caught my attention as a writer and observer.

I have watched a marked polarization in U.S. society. As court decisions and the general drift of culture push religion to the fringe, some Christians act more and more as if they belong to a fringe religion. Christians under duress often show a tendency to withdraw from the world, pull up the drawbridge, and retreat behind a protective moat. I feel sad about this trend because it directly contradicts Jesus' command to act like salt in meat and light in the midst of darkness. Salt has no effect when sealed in a jar on the shelf, and a closeted lamp illuminates nothing.

The "castle" into which Christians retreat is the church. That makes me sad as well, because for many people the church can be the least likely place to find God. Jesus himself looked for God not among the pious at the synagogue, but in a widow who had two pennies left to her name and in a tax collector who knew no formal prayers; he found his spiritual lessons in sparrows sold at a market, and in wheat fields and wedding banquets, and, yes, even in the observations of a mixed-race foreigner who had five failed marriages. Jesus was a master at finding God in unexpected places.

In my own pilgrimage, I have had to look beyond church walls in order to find God. Growing up in Southern fundamentalism, my search for God was blocked by racism and fear and judgment. In the beautiful, orderly world of nature I first saw glimpses of a Creator who has lavished on us a good and grace-filled world. As I began to believe, I found rumors of transcendence—the footprints of God—in places I had never before thought of looking.

Theologian John S. Dunne tells of a group of early Spanish sailors who reached the continent of South America after an arduous voyage. Their caravels sailed into the headwaters of the Amazon, an expanse of water so wide the sailors presumed it to be a continuation of the Atlantic Ocean. It never occurred to them to drink the water, since they expected it to be saline, and as a result some of these sailors died of thirst. That scene of men dying of thirst even as their ships floated on the world's largest source of freshwater has become for me a metaphor for our age. Some people starve to death spiritually while all around them manna rots.

People shake their heads in despair over the state of the world despite the fact that by many measures—literacy, nutrition, clean water, housing—things have decidedly improved in the past fifty years. Toward the end of the last century, one-third of all people on earth gained freedom from perhaps the greatest tyranny in history, with hardly a shot being fired. In Eastern Europe, a god fell to earth like an idol pulled from its pedestal, and at its base stood Christians armed with candles and the power of prayer. In South Africa, the leader of the last theologically racist party on earth led the way toward reconciliation. Why the change? F. W. de Klerk himself gave the reason: after his inauguration, in tears, he told his church that he had felt a calling from God to save all the people of South Africa, even though he knew he would be rejected by his own people. In China, the greatest revival of faith in history broke out in an atheistic state that tried desperately to quell it.

We tend to see what we are looking for. At the time the microscope was first invented, scientists believed that sperm were little embryos, with the woman serving as an incubator. Peering through the early microscopes, they saw and drew those embryos, *homunculi* or "little men." They saw what they expected to see. Similarly, when the great astronomer Percival Lowell got a new twenty-four-inch telescope on a mountain in Flagstaff, Arizona, he "saw" a network of canals on Mars that confirmed the theories of Italian astronomers. He mapped them on a globe, and his 1908 book *Mars as the Abode of Life* laid out proof that these canals were built by intelligent beings.

Sometimes, like Lowell, we see things that aren't really there and sometimes, like the Spanish sailors, we fail to notice the very element we're floating in. In the world of faith, particularly, some things have to be believed to be seen.

The job of a journalist is, simply, to see. We are professional eyes. As a Christian journalist, I have learned to look for traces of God. I have found those traces in unexpected places: among the chief propagandists of a formerly atheistic nation and refugees from a currently atheistic nation; in a storefront chapel at Ground Zero, an Atlanta slum, and even a Chicago health club; at a meeting of Amnesty International, on a weekend retreat with twenty Jews and Muslims, and on a panel addressing "Why Do Muslims Hate Us?"; in the prisons of Peru and Chile and orphanages in South Africa and Myanmar; in the speeches of Vaclav Havel and even in the plays of Shakespeare. This book, much of it adapted from my occasional writings, is my report of what I have seen in recent years.

I have found malaise in the midst of plenty and stirring hope in circumstances that should have produced despair. I have found evil in the most unexpected places, and also God.

This book was first published in 1995, but after 2001 the world changed so much I felt the need for a revision. In 1995 the economy was booming, the Cold War was a fast-receding memory, and the United States stood virtually unchallenged. Now everyone who goes through an airport security line or opens a suspicious-looking envelope knows that the world has changed. Fear now reigns. I removed nine chapters that seemed relevant before September 11, 2001, but less so afterward, and added fourteen new ones, including an entire section on "Finding God in the Rubble."

I do not ask you to believe all that I believe, or to walk the same path I have walked. All I ask is that you keep an open mind as you look at the world through my eyes.

On a trip to South Africa, I met a remarkable woman named Joanna. She is of mixed race, part black and part white, a category known there as "Coloured." As a student she agitated for change in apartheid and then saw the miracle that no one had predicted, the peaceful dismantling of that evil system. Afterward, for many hours she sat with her husband and watched live broadcasts of the Truth and Reconciliation Commission hearings.

Instead of simply exulting in her newfound freedoms, Joanna next decided to tackle the most violent prison in South Africa, a prison where Nelson Mandela had spent several years. Tattoo-covered gang members controlled the prison, strictly enforcing a rule that required new members to earn their admittance to the gang by assaulting undesirable prisoners. Prison authorities looked the other way, letting these "animals" beat and even kill each other.

Alone, this attractive young woman started going each day into the bowels of that prison. She brought a simple message of forgiveness and reconciliation, trying to put into practice on a smaller scale what Mandela and Bishop Tutu were trying to effect in the nation as a whole. She organized small groups, taught trust games, got the prisoners to open up about the details of their horrific childhoods. The year before she began her visits, the prison had recorded 279 acts of violence; the next year there were two. Joanna's results were so impressive that the BBC sent a camera crew from London to produce two one-hour documentaries on her.

I met Joanna and her husband, who has since joined her in the prison work, at a restaurant on the waterfront of Cape Town. Ever the journalist, I pressed her for specifics on what had happened to transform that prison. Her fork stopped on the way to her mouth, she looked up and said, almost without thinking, "Well, of course, Philip, God was already present in the prison. I just had to make him visible."

I have often thought of that line from Joanna, which would make a fine mission statement for all of us seeking to know and follow God. God is already present, in the most unexpected places. We just need to make God visible.

Philip Yancey

## Part One

✠

# Finding

# God

# Without

# Really

# Looking

Chapter 1

# Rumors of Another World

According to Greek mythology, people once knew in advance their exact day of death. Everyone on earth lived with a deep sense of melancholy, for mortality hung like a sword suspended above them. All that changed when Prometheus introduced the gift of fire. Now humans could reach beyond themselves to control their destinies; they could strive to be like the gods. Caught up in excitement over these new possibilities, people soon lost the knowledge of their death day.

Have we moderns lost even more? Have we lost, in fact, the sense that we will die at all?

Although some authors argue as much (such as social theorist Ernest Becker in *The Denial of Death*), I have found that behind the noise of daily life, rumors of another world can still be heard. The whispers of death persist, and I have heard them, I believe, in three unlikely places: a health club, a political action group, and a hospital therapy group. I have even detected the overtones—but only overtones—of theology in these unexpected places.

I joined the Chicago Health Club after a foot injury forced me to find alternatives to running. It took a while to adjust to the artificiality of the place. Patrons lined up to use high-tech rowing machines, complete with video screens and animation pace boats, though Lake Michigan, a real lake requiring real oars, lay empty just four blocks away. In another room, people working out at StairMaster machines duplicated the act of climbing stairs—this in a dense patch of high-rise buildings. And I marveled at the technology that adds computer-programmed excitement to the everyday feat of bicycling.

I marveled, too, at the human bodies using all these machines: the gorgeous women wearing black and hot pink leotards, and the huge hunks of masculinity who clustered around the weight machines. Mirrored glass, appropriately, sheathed the walls, and a quick glance revealed dozens of eyes checking out the results of all the sweating and grunting, on themselves and on their neighbors.

The health club is a modern temple, complete with initiation rites and elaborate rituals, its objects of worship on constant and glorious display. I detected a trace of theology there, for such devotion to the human form gives evidence of the genius of a Creator who designed with aesthetic flair. The human person is worth preserving. And yet, in the end, the health club stands as a pagan temple. Its members strive to preserve only one part of the person: the body, the least enduring part of all.

Ernest Becker wrote his book and died before the exercise craze gripped America, but I imagine he would see in health clubs a blatant symptom of death-denial. Health clubs, along with cosmetic surgery, baldness retardants, skin creams, and an endless proliferation of magazines on sports, swimsuits, and dieting help direct our attention away from death toward life. Life in this body. And if we all strive together to preserve our bodies, then perhaps science will one day achieve the unthinkable: perhaps it will conquer mortality and permit us to live forever, like Gulliver's toothless, hairless, memoryless race of Struldbruggs.

Once, as I was pedaling nowhere on a computerized bicycle, I thought of Kierkegaard's comment that the knowledge of one's own death is the essential fact that distinguishes us from animals. I looked around the exercise room wondering just how distinguished from the animals we modern humans are. The frenzied activity I was participating in at that moment—was it merely one more way of denying or postponing death? As a nation, do we grow sleek and healthy so that we do not have to think about the day our muscular bodies will be, not pumping iron, but lying stiff in a casket?

Martin Luther told his followers, "Even in the best of health we should have death always before our eyes [so that] we will not expect to remain on this earth forever, but will have one foot in the air, so to speak." His words seem quaint indeed today when most of us, pagan and Christian alike, spend out days thinking about everything but death. Even the church focuses mainly on the good that faith can offer *now:* physical health, inner peace, financial security, a stable marriage.

Physical training is of some value, the apostle Paul advised his protégé Timothy, but godliness has value for all things, holding promise for both the present life and the life to come. As I pedaled, straining against computer-generated hills, I had to ask myself: What is my spiritual counterpart to the Chicago Health Club? And then, more troubling: How much time and energy do I devote to each?

For two years I attended monthly meetings of a local chapter of Amnesty International. There I met good people, serious people: students and executives and professionals who gather together because they find it intolerable blithely to go on with life while other people are being tortured and killed.

Amnesty International's local chapters use an absurdly simple technique to combat human rights abuses: they write letters. Our group adopted three prisoners of conscience, all of whom were serving long-term sentences for "unpatriotic activity." Each week we would discuss their fates and report on the letters we had written to esteemed officials in their respective countries.

As we sat in a comfortable townhouse eating brownies and fresh vegetables and sipping coffee, we tried to envision how Jorge and Ahmad and Joseph were spending their days and evenings. Letters from their families gave us agonizing insight into their hardships. Despite our efforts to resist it, most of the time a vague feeling of powerlessness pervaded the room. We had received no word from Jorge in two years, and officials in his South American country no longer answered our letters. Most likely he had joined "the disappeared."

The tone of earnest concern in the group reminded me of many prayer meetings I had attended. Those, too, focused group energy on specific human needs. Yet at Amnesty International no one dared pray, a fact that perhaps added to the sense of helplessness. Although the organization was founded on Christian principles, any trace of sectarianism had long since disappeared.

Here is a strange thing, I thought one evening. A worthy organization exists for the sole purpose of keeping people alive. Thousands of bright, dedicated people congregate in small groups centered on that singular goal. But one question is never addressed: *Why* should we keep people alive?

I have asked that question of Amnesty International staff members, provoking a response of quiet horror. The very phrasing of the question seemed heretical to them. Why keep people alive? The answer is self-evident, is it not? Life is good; death is bad (I presume they meant animal life is good, since we were munching vegetable life as we spoke).

These staff members missed the irony that Amnesty International came into existence because not all people in history see their equation as self-evident. To Hitler, to Stalin, to Saddam Hussein, death can be a good if it helps accomplish other goals. No ultimate value attaches to any one human life.

Amnesty International recognizes the inherent worth of every human being. Unlike, say, the Chicago Health Club, AI does not elevate beautiful specimens of perfect health: the objects of our attention were mostly bruised and beaten, with missing teeth and unkempt hair and signs of malnutrition. But what makes such people worthy of our care? To put it bluntly, is it possible to honor the image of God in a human being if there is no God?

To raise such questions at an Amnesty International meeting is to invite a time of stern and awkward silence. Explanations may follow. *This is not a religious organization. . . . We cannot deal with such sectarian views. . . . People have differing opinions. . . . The important issue is the fate of our prisoners. . . .*

In our strange society, it seems the questions most worth asking are the questions most ignored. The French mathematician Blaise Pascal lived during the seventeenth-century Enlightenment era, when Western thinkers first began scorning belief in a soul and the afterlife, matters of doctrine that seemed to them primitive and unsophisticated. Pascal said of such people, "Do they profess to have delighted us by telling us that they hold our soul to be only a little wind and smoke, especially by telling us this in a haughty and self-satisfied tone of voice? Is this a thing to say gaily? Is it not, on the contrary, a thing to say sadly, as the saddest thing in the world?"

I still belong to Amnesty International and contribute money to it. I believe in their cause, but I believe in it for different reasons. Why do strangers such as Ahmad and Joseph and Jorge deserve my time and energy? I can think of only one reason: that they bear the sign of ultimate worth, the image of God.

Amnesty International teaches a more advanced theology than the Chicago Health Club, to be sure. It points past the surface of skin and shape to the inner person. But the organization stops short—for what makes the inner person worth preserving, unless it be a soul? And for that very reason, shouldn't Christians lead the way in such issues as human rights? According to the Bible, all humans, including Jorge and Ahmad and Joseph, are immortal beings who still bear some mark of the Creator.

Members of the Chicago Health Club do their best to defy or at least forestall death. Amnesty International works diligently to prevent it. But another group I attended faces death head-on, once a month.

I was first invited to Make Today Count, a support group for people with life-threatening illnesses, by my neighbor Jim, who had just been diagnosed with terminal cancer. There we met other people, mostly in their thirties, who were battling such diseases as multiple sclerosis, hepatitis, muscular dystrophy, and cancer. For each member of the group, all of life had boiled down to two issues: surviving and, failing that, preparing for death.

We sat in a hospital waiting area on molded plastic chairs of a garish orange hue (doubtless chosen to make the institution appear more cheerful). We tried to ignore the loudspeaker periodically crackling out an announcement or paging a doctor. The meeting began with each member "checking in." Jim whispered to me this was the most depressing part of the meeting, because very often someone had died in the month since the last meeting. The social worker provided details of the missing member's last days and the funeral.

The members of Make Today Count confronted death because they had no choice. I had expected a mood of great somberness, but found just the opposite. Tears flowed freely, of course, but these people spoke easily and comfortably about disease and death. Clearly, the group was the one place they could talk openly about such issues.

Nancy showed off a new wig, purchased to cover the baldness caused by chemotherapy treatments. She joked that she had always wanted straight hair, and now her brain tumor had finally given her an excuse. Steve, a young man with Hodgkin's disease, admitted he was terrified of what lay ahead. His fiancée refused to discuss the future with him at all. How could he break through to her?

Martha talked about death. The disease ALS ("Lou Gehrig's disease") had already rendered her legs and arms useless. Now she breathed with great difficulty, and whenever she fell asleep at night there was a danger of death from oxygen deprivation. Martha was twenty-five years old. "What is it you fear about death?" someone asked. Martha thought a minute and then said this, "I regret all that I'm going to miss—next year's big movies, for example, and the election results. And I fear that I will one day be forgotten. That I'll just disappear, and no one will even miss me."

More than any other people I have met, members of the Make Today Count group concentrated on ultimate issues. They, unlike the Chicago Health Clubbers, could not deny death; their bodies bore memento mori, reminders of inevitable, premature death. Every day they were, in Saint Augustine's phrase, "deafened by the clanking chains of mortality." I wanted to use them as examples for my hedonistic friends, to walk down the street and interrupt parties to announce, "We're all going to die. I have proof. Just around the corner is a place where you can see it for yourself. Have you thought about death?"

Yet would such awareness change anyone for more than a few minutes? As one of novelist Saul Bellow's characters put it, the living speed like birds over the surface of the water, and one will dive or plunge but not come up again and never be seen again. But life goes on. Five thousand people die in America each day.

One night Donna, a member of the Make Today Count group, told about watching a television program on the public service station. In the program, Elisabeth Kübler-Ross discussed a boy in Switzerland who was dying of an inoperable brain tumor. Kübler-Ross asked him to draw a picture of how he felt. He drew a large, ugly military tank, and behind the tank he drew a small house with trees, grass, sunshine, and an open window. In front of the tank, just at the end of the gun barrel, he drew a tiny figure with a red stop sign in his hand. Himself.

Donna said that picture captured her feelings precisely. Kübler-Ross had gone on to describe the five stages of grief, culminating in the stage of acceptance. And Donna knew she was supposed to work toward acceptance. But she could never get past the stage of fear. Like the little boy in front of the tank, she saw death as an enemy.

Someone brought up religious faith and belief in an afterlife, but the comment evoked the same response in Make Today Count as it had in Amnesty International: a long silence, a cleared throat, a few rolled eyes. The rest of the evening, the group focused on how Donna could overcome her fears and grow toward the acceptance stage of grief.

I left that meeting with a heavy heart. Our materialistic, undogmatic culture was asking its members to defy their deepest feelings. Donna and the small Swiss boy with the brain tumor had, by sheer primal instinct, struck upon a cornerstone of Christian theology. Death is an enemy, a grievous enemy, the last enemy to be destroyed. How could members of a group that each month saw families fall apart and bodies deteriorate before their eyes still wish for a spirit of bland acceptance? I could think of only one appropriate response to Donna's impending death: *Curse you, death!*

There was another aspect of Christian theology, too, the one, most sadly, that Make Today Count would not discuss. The Swiss boy had included his vision of Heaven in the background, represented by the grass and trees and the cottage with an open window. Any feeling like "acceptance" would be appropriate only if he was truly going somewhere, somewhere like home. That is why I consider the doctrine of Heaven one of the most neglected doctrines of our time.

"I think it is very hard for secular men to die," said Ernest Becker, as he turned to God in the last months of his life.

In the Prado museum in Madrid, Spain, there hangs a painting by Hans Baldung (d. 1545) titled *The Stages of Life, with Death*. It seems a deliberate parody of the classical image of *The Three Graces*. On the ground lies a newborn child, resting peacefully. Three pale, elongated figures stand over the child. On the left is a nearly nude woman, the archetype of classical beauty, her skin like alabaster, her figure round and smooth, her hair braided into long strands that cascade down her back. To her left stands an old hag with shriveled, sagging breasts and a sharp, angular face. The hag has her right hand on the beautiful woman's shoulder and, with a mocking, toothless sneer, is pulling the young woman toward her.

The hag's left arm is interlocked with that of a third person, a horrid figure straight out of Hieronymus Bosch, the medieval painter with a passion for the grotesque. Man or woman, you cannot tell. Human features have melted down in a macabre, rotting corpse, with long, slender worms crawling out of its cadaver belly. The head is hairless, nearly a skull. The corpse holds an hourglass.

Hans Baldung's painting restores, visually, what humanity lost after Prometheus. The beautiful woman has regained the knowledge of the hour of death. Birth, youth, old age—we live out each stage under death's shadow.

The painting lacks one image, a vision of a resurrected body. It is hard for us to live in awareness of death; it may be even harder to live in awareness of afterlife. We hope for re-created bodies while inhabiting aged and ailing ones. Charles Williams, the novelist and friend of C. S. Lewis, once admitted that the notion of immortality never seemed to stir his imagination, no matter how hard he tried. "Our experience on earth makes it difficult for us to apprehend a good without a catch in it somewhere," he said.

The apostle Paul wrote these words to people who, like us, could not quite imagine a good without a catch in it somewhere:

> Though outwardly we are wasting away [*despite all attempts at the Chicago Health Club to reverse entropy*], yet inwardly we are being renewed day by day. For our light and momentary troubles [*Light and momentary! Paul's jailings, beatings, and shipwrecks remind me of the stories of tortured prisoners I hear about at Amnesty International*] are achieving for us an eternal glory that far outweighs them all. So we fix our eyes not on what is seen, but on what is unseen. For what is seen is temporary, but what is unseen is eternal.
>
> . . . For while we are in this tent, we groan [*drawn, haggard, chemotherapied faces from the Make Today Count group come to mind*], and are burdened, because we do not wish to be unclothed but to be clothed with our heavenly dwelling, so that what is mortal may be swallowed up by life. Now it is God who has made us for this very purpose and has given us the Spirit as a deposit, guaranteeing what is to come. (2 Corinthians 4:16–5:5)

We need a renewed awareness of death, yes. But we need far more. We need a faith, in the midst of our groaning, that death is not the last word, but the next to last. What is mortal will be swallowed up by life. One day all whispers of death will fall silent.

# Chapter 2

# Not Naked Enough

When I moved into the city of Chicago from the suburbs, I was surprised to find the urban atmosphere more sexually charged. Downtown health clubs, billboards, magazine racks, porno shops, and street wear all revealed, well, *more*. Much more.

It seems curious that a culture advancing in sophistication and technology should heighten the emphasis on sexuality, the primal drive that humans share with all animals, but in my travels I have noticed this consistent pattern. In the Amazon jungle, sex has its place, surely, but it ranks somewhere below a successful hunt or a communal feast. In New York or Paris or Tokyo, sex is sine qua non, the Prime Mover that advertisers rely on in order to sell fine wine, computers, and dental floss.

Whenever a Christian writer turns to the subject of sex, I realize, certain defenses go up. Readers expect a moralistic screed against the sex excess in modern society. I, for one, see little value in such an approach. In the first place, moralizing doesn't stand much chance against the raw power of human sexual drives.

More important, I wonder whether the church has used the wrong approach toward sex entirely. Too often the church has treated sexuality as a grave threat, a rival to spirituality. If you're oversexed, why, repress your sexuality and sublimate that energy into a longing for God. Between the third and tenth centuries, church authorities issued edicts forbidding sex on Saturdays, Wednesdays, and Fridays, and also during the forty-day fast periods before Easter, Christmas, and Whitsuntide, all for religious reasons. They kept adding feast days and days of the apostles to the proscription as well as the days of female impurity until it reached the point that, as historian John Boswell has estimated, only forty-four days a year remained available for marital sex. Human nature being what it is, the church's proscriptions were enthusiastically ignored.

I question the motive behind such edicts. Can we so neatly substitute one drive (toward spiritual union) for another (toward physical union)? I doubt it. After all, in the Garden of Eden, when prelapsarian Adam had perfect spiritual communion with God, even then he felt a loneliness and longing that met no relief until God created Eve.

Rather than positioning sexuality and spirituality against each other as rivals, I see them as deeply related. The more I observe our society's obsession with sexuality, the more I sense in it a thirst for transcendence.

My urban neighbors in their condominiums and high-rises and even those in the suburbs have little transcendence left in their lives. Few of them attend church; they believe science has figured out most of the numinous mysteries of the universe, like disease and weather. Except for the New Agers among them, they tend to scoff at superstitious practices like astrology.

But sex—ah, there's a mystery to which normal principles of reductionism do not apply. Sex is not something you can "figure out." Knowing about sex, even taking a degree in gynecology, doesn't diminish its magical power. Probably the closest thing to a supernatural experience my male neighbors ever have is when they watch Catherine Zeta-Jones in a clingy red dress, or when they pore over each microdot of the annual *Sports Illustrated* swimsuit issue. Is it any wonder these swimsuit models are often called "goddesses"?

In this view, sex is not a rival to spirituality, but rather a pointer to it. When a society so completely blocks the human thirst for transcendence, should we be surprised that such longings reroute themselves into an expression of mere physicality? Maybe the problem is not that people are getting naked, but that they aren't getting naked enough: we stop at the skin instead of going deeper, into the soul.

I once talked with the priest Henri Nouwen just after he had returned from San Francisco. He had visited various ministries to people with AIDS and was moved with compassion by sad stories of sexual promiscuity. "They want love so badly that it's killing them—literally," he said.

More and more, I see sex excess as a modern mutation of classical idolatry, a commitment of spirit to something that cannot bear its weight. When God rebuked the Israelites for their idolatry, he was not condemning their urge to worship. Nor did he disapprove of the more immediate urges that pushed them toward idols: a desire for fertility, for good weather, for military success. Rather, he condemned them for seeking those things from senseless hunks of wood and iron instead of from himself.

What the Old Testament calls idolatry, enlightened Westerners call "addictions." These, too, are often good things—sex, food, work, chocolate—that outgrow their rightful place and begin to control a person's life. To a member of AA, alcohol represents an "idol" in which he or she invests all hopes and dreams. The idol of alcohol, like the golden calf, cannot bear such total commitment. It always lets you down.

Tellingly, even our secularized society has found but one effective way to break the pattern of addiction: twelve-step programs, all of which require submission to a "Higher Power." In their own desperate ways, these strugglers are searching for an elixir that will quench their thirst for transcendence.

The French priest Jean Sulivan made this observation about modern society: "Human beings are not looking for just anything but for the absolute, even when they believe they are turning away from it, or when they unknowingly repress it in a search for material things." Repression of spirituality is every bit as dangerous as repression of sexuality.

I was thinking some of these thoughts as I read again the account of Jesus' conversation with a Samaritan woman who had been through five husbands and was living with yet another man. Two things struck me. First, I was reminded of Jesus' exquisite tenderness in dealing with people who had failed on some level. In those days the husband initiated divorce: this Samaritan woman had been unceremoniously dumped by five different men.

I was also struck by Jesus' skill in connecting thirst—physical, parched-throat thirst and also the thirst for intimacy—with a thirst for transcendence that only he could satisfy. "Everyone who drinks this water will be thirsty again, but whoever drinks the water I give him will never thirst," he said.

This Samaritan "outcast" woman was the first person to whom Jesus openly revealed himself as the Messiah. After the conversation by a well, this same woman led a wholesale revival in her town. When her deepest thirst was quenched, a thirst she had never even recognized before Jesus named it, all other thirsts took their rightful place.

# Chapter 3

# The Lost Sex Survey

While much of the media was buzzing about a new survey on sex in modern America released in 1994, I was thinking about a book, *Sex and Culture*, published in 1934. I discovered it in the windowless warrens of a large university library, and I felt like an archaeologist must feel unearthing an artifact from the catacombs.

Seeking to test the Freudian notion that civilization is a by-product of repressed sexuality, the scholar J. D. Unwin studied eighty-six different societies. His findings startled many scholars, above all Unwin himself, because all eighty-six demonstrated a direct tie between absolute monogamy and the "expansive energy" of civilization. In other words, sexual fidelity was the single most important predictor of a society's ascendancy.

Unwin had no religious convictions and applied no moral judgment. "I offer no opinion about rightness or wrongness." Nevertheless, he had to conclude, "In human records there is no instance of a society retaining its energy after a complete new generation has inherited a tradition which does not insist on prenuptial and post-nuptial continence."

For Roman, Greek, Sumerian, Moorish, Babylonian, and Anglo-Saxon civilizations, Unwin had several hundred years of history to draw on. He found with no exceptions that these societies flourished, culturally and geographically, during eras that valued sexual fidelity. Inevitably, sexual mores would loosen and the societies would subsequently decline, only to rise again when they returned to more rigid sexual standards.

Unwin seemed at a loss to explain the pattern. "If you ask me why this is so, I reply that I do not know. No scientist does. . . . You can describe the process and observe it, but you cannot explain it." Yet the trend so impressed him that he proposed a special class of "Alpha" citizens in Great Britain. These individuals of unusual promise would take vows of chastity before marriage and observe strict monogamy after marriage, all for the sake of the empire, which needed their talents.

Unwin died before fully developing his theory on "the sexual foundations of a new society," but the incomplete results were published in another book, *Hopousia,* with an introduction by Aldous Huxley.

A decade before Unwin did his research, followers of Vladimir Lenin were espousing a very different "glass of water" theory about sex. Sexual desire is no more mysterious or sacrosanct than the desire for food or water, they declared, and rewrote the Soviet lawbook accordingly. That theory soon collapsed and Soviet society became—on the surface at least—almost puritanical about sexual morality.

Today we hear new versions of the glass of water theory. "Sex can finally, after all these centuries, be separated from the all-too-serious business of reproduction," proclaimed Barbara Ehrenreich in a *Time* essay. She gets specific: ". . . what could be more moral than teaching that homosexuality is a viable life-style? Or that masturbation is harmless and normal? Or that petting, under most circumstances, makes far more sense than begetting? The only ethic that can work in an overcrowded world is one that insists that women are free, children are loved, and sex—preferably among affectionate and consenting adults—belongs squarely in the realm of play."

Ehrenreich's call for the "de-moralization" of sex has about it the incense smell of the 1960s, birth era of the modern sexual revolution. AIDS may have temporarily dampened enthusiasm for unrestrained lovemaking, but I hear few social commentators articulating a coherent sexual ethic. In our reductionist society, sex is viewed as a purely biological act, like drinking and eating. Once we perfect the technology of protection, we can go back to coupling.

(Strangely, though, sex resists reductionism. Jealousy still rears its ugly head and cuckolds still murder their lovers' lovers, as if sexuality involved the joining of lives and not merely genitals. And in an age of unprecedented birth control options and widespread sex education, our society produces more unwanted pregnancies than ever before.)

Frankly, I do not know what to make of J. D. Unwin's theories about sex and culture. His books rest in the catacombs of libraries because he preached a message that few want to hear, and his moral basis for fidelity ("Zip up for the empire!") easily gets overwhelmed by sheer hormonal force. Moreover, his criterion of "expansive energy" looks different in an age that frowns on imperialism.

Without realizing it, though, Unwin may have subtly edged toward a Christian view of sexuality from which modern society has badly strayed. For the Christian, sex is not an end in itself, but rather a gift from God. Like all such gifts, it must be stewarded according to God's rules, not ours.

If we make a god of progress and destroy the planet God gave us to steward, we will destroy ourselves as well. If we worship power and success and construct the greatest civilization the world has ever seen—it too will fall, as Unwin's Babelic survey of history surely shows. And if we make a god of sexuality, that god will also fail, in ways that affect the whole person and perhaps the whole society.

Author Bruce Marshall once said that a man who rings the bell at the brothel is unconsciously looking for God. That statement has always reminded me of Jesus' conversation with the Samaritan woman at the well, in which he used her thirst for love to introduce her to Living Water.

We have two conflicting ways to look at sex, and each involves a paradox. The reductionist glass of water theory unexpectedly elevates sexuality to a place it does not deserve and cannot sustain; as we give it worship, society disintegrates. On the other hand, the Living Water theory ennobles what at first it seems to dethrone, by restoring sex to its rightful place, as a gift of transcendental value.

# Chapter 4

# Looking Up

I have been thinking about the universe lately. The whole thing. After reading some of astronomer Chet Raymo's elegiac prose *(Starry Nights, The Soul of the Night)*, I have been craning my neck upward at odd angles.

Learning about the universe does little for earthly self-esteem. Our sun, powerful enough to turn white skin bronze and coax oxygen from every plant on earth, ranks fairly low by galactic standards. If the giant star Antares were positioned where our sun is—93 million miles away—the earth would be inside it! And our sun and Antares represent just two of 400 billion stars that swim around in the vast, forlorn space of the Milky Way. A dime held out at arm's length would block 15 million stars from view, if our eyes could see with unlimited power.

From our hemisphere, only one other galaxy, Andromeda, is large enough and close enough (a mere 2 million light years away) to see with the naked eye. It showed up on star charts long before the invention of the telescope, and until recently no one could know that the little blob of light marked the presence of another galaxy, one twice the size of the Milky Way and home to half a trillion stars. Or that these next-door neighbors were but two of 100 billion galaxies likewise swarming with stars.

One reason the night sky stays dark despite the presence of so many luminous bodies is that all the galaxies are hurtling away from each other with astonishing speed. Tomorrow, some galaxies will be 30 million miles farther away from us. In the time it takes to type this sentence, they'll have receded another 5,100 miles.

I saw the Milky Way in full glory once, while visiting a refugee camp in Somalia, just below the equator. Our galaxy stretched across the canopy of darkness like a highway paved with diamond dust. Since that night, when I lay with warm sand at my back far from the nearest streetlight, the sky has never seemed as empty and the earth never as large.

I had spent all day interviewing relief workers about the mega-disaster of the moment. Kurdistan, Rwanda, Sudan, Ethiopia— place names change, but the spectacle of suffering has a dreary sameness: mothers with shriveled, milkless breasts, babies crying and dying, fathers foraging for firewood in a treeless terrain.

After three days of hearing tales of human misery, I could not lift my sights beyond that refugee camp situated in an obscure corner of an obscure country on the Horn of Africa. Until I saw the Milky Way. It abruptly reminded me that the present moment did not comprise all of life. History would go on. Tribes, governments, whole civilizations may rise and fall, trailing disaster in their wake, but I dared not confine my field of vision to the scenes of suffering around me. I needed to look up, to the stars.

"Can you bind the beautiful Pleiades? Can you loose the cords of Orion? Can you bring forth the constellations in the seasons or lead out the Bear with its cubs? Do you know the laws of the heavens? Can you set up God's dominion over the earth?" These questions God asked a man named Job who, obsessed with his own great pain, had confined his vision to the borders of his itchy skin. Remarkably, God's reminder seemed to help Job. His skin still itched, but Job got a glimpse of other matters God must attend to in a universe of 100 billion galaxies.

To me, God's speech in the Book of Job conveys a tone of gruffness. But perhaps that is its most important message: the Lord of the Universe has a right to gruffness when assailed by one tiny human being, notwithstanding the merits of his complaint. We descendants of Job dare not lose sight of the Big Picture, a sight best glimpsed on moonless, starry nights.

You can almost mark the advancement of a people by noting their interest in stargazing. Each great civilization of the past—Inca, Moghul, Chinese, Egyptian, Greek, Renaissance European—made major breakthroughs in astronomy. There is an irony at work in human history: one by one, civilizations gain the capacity to fathom their own insignificance, then fail to recognize that fact and fade away.

What about us, we launchers of the Viking and Apollo spacecrafts, we makers of the orbiting Hubble observatory, Mars rovers, and the Very Large Array radio telescopes strewn over thirty-nine miles of New Mexico desert? Do our achievements make us more, or less, humble? More, or less, worshipful?

About the same time I read Chet Raymo, I went to see a film taken by a Space Shuttle crew with a special format OMNIMAX camera. The lightning storms impressed me most. Viewed from space, lightning flashes on and off in a random pattern of beauty, illuminating cloud cover several hundred miles wide at a burst. It flares, spreads across an expanse, glows, then pales. Most eerily, it makes no sound.

I was struck by the huge difference perspective makes. On earth, families huddled indoors, cars hid under highway overpasses, animals cowered in the forest, children cried out in the night. Transformers sparked, creeks flooded, dogs howled. But from space we saw only a soft, pleasant glow, enlarging then retreating, an ocean tide of light.

Chet Raymo, who sleeps in the day and stares upward at night, lives with a constant sense of wonder, a by-product of observing the universe. He describes how the receding galaxies point back to a Big Bang of creation in which all the matter of the universe came into existence in a giant explosion that lasted one second. He acknowledges the unimaginable odds against anything good coming out of such an explosion by chance: "If, one second after the Big Bang, the ratio of the density of the universe to its expansion rate had differed from its assumed value by only one part in $10^{15}$ (that's 1 followed by fifteen zeros), the universe would have either quickly collapsed upon itself or ballooned so rapidly that stars and galaxies could not have condensed from the primal matter. . . . If all the grains of sand on all the beaches of the earth were possible universes—that is, universes consistent with the laws of physics as we know them—and only one of those grains of sand were a universe that allowed for the existence of intelligent life, then that one grain of sand is the universe we inhabit."

After reading Chet Raymo, I turned to a passage I had marked long ago in the extraordinary book *Alone*, Commander Richard Byrd's account of a six-month sojourn of solitude in Antarctica near the South Pole. Byrd often found himself looking up; all other landscape was blank white. Living farther south than any human being, he witnessed things in the sky—such as refraction phenomena that shot bands of color through the sun's core—visible to no one else on earth.

After one chilly afternoon stroll (it was 89 degrees below zero in the season of perpetual night), he sat down and wrote about what he had seen stargazing during many such walks. "The conviction came that rhythm was too orderly, too harmonious, too perfect to be a product of blind chance—that, therefore, there must be purpose in the whole and that man was part of that whole and not an accidental offshoot. It was a feeling that transcended reason; that went to the heart of man's despair and found it groundless. The universe was a cosmos, not a chaos; man was as rightfully a part of that cosmos as were the day, and night."

It takes great effort, and considerable faith, to keep the Big Picture in mind. In some ways it makes me feel utterly insignificant, in some ways eternally significant. If the God who engineered creation with such precision professes some whit of interest in what takes place on this speck of a planet, the least I can do is wander away from the streetlights more often and look up.

Chapter 5

# Of Whales and Polar Bears

*Earth is crammed with heaven*
*And every bush aflame with God*
*But only those who see take off their shoes.*
—ELIZABETH BARRETT BROWNING

I admit that I'm a soft touch for the Argument from Design. For me, the world of nature bears spectacular witness to the imaginative genius of our Creator. Consider these examples that I encountered on a trip to Alaska.

- A nearly invisible ice fish swims among the icebergs of Arctic and Antarctic waters, its survival made possible by the unique properties of its blood. A special protein acts as an antifreeze to keep ice crystals from forming, and its blood has no hemoglobin or red pigment. As a result, the fish is virtually transparent.
- The instinctive navigational ability of common ducks, geese, and swans makes them the envy of the aircraft industry. On their trips south, some of the geese maintain a speed of fifty miles per hour and fly a thousand miles before making their first rest stop.

• When it comes to navigation, polar bears are no slouches, either. A polar bear that is tranquilized, trapped, and released three hundred miles away can usually find its way home, even across drift ice that changes constantly and holds no landmarks and few odors. But bears and birds are rank amateurs compared to lowly salmon, who cruise the expanse of the Pacific Ocean for several years before returning (by scent? magnetic field?) to the streams of their birth.

• Baby musk oxen are born in March and April, when temperatures still languish around 30 degrees below zero. Thus, as the tiny musk ox drops two feet to the ground, its surrounding temperature drops 130 degrees. The mother must hasten to lick blood and fluid from the coat of the steaming calf lest it freeze. Within a few minutes, the calf staggers to its feet and begins to nurse.

• Comparatively, mother grizzlies and polar bears have it easy. Ursine mothers feel no pain when giving birth for the simple reason that birthing takes place in the dead of winter, hibernation time. The cub struggles through the birth canal, pokes around the new world, and figures out the nursing process on its own. (Imagine the mother bear's surprise when spring rolls around.)

• One more fact about polar bears. For years it puzzled researchers that polar bears and harp seals never showed up on the aerial infrared photographs used in animal censuses. Yet both species showed up very dark on ultraviolet photographs, even though white objects normally reflect, rather than absorb, ultraviolet light rays. In 1978 a U.S. Army researcher discovered the reason. Polar bear hairs are not white at all, but transparent. Under a scanning electron microscope they appear as hollow tubes, without pigment. They act like tiny fiber-optic tubes, trapping the warming ultraviolet rays and

funneling them to the bear's body. At the same time the
fur provides such efficient insulation that the bear's outer
temperature stays virtually the same as the surrounding
ice—which explains why bears do not show up on
infrared photos.

When I learn such details about the natural world, I feel like
writing a hymn in honor of the polar bear or musk ox. Such a
hymn would have good precedent: in his majestic speech at the
end of the Book of Job, God himself pointed to the wonders of
creation as compelling proof of his power and wisdom. When he
and Job compared résumés, Job ended up repenting in dust and
ashes.

As I say, I'm a soft touch for the Argument from Design. Still,
I must acknowledge that not everyone responds to nature in the
same way. As novelist Walker Percy has observed, "There may be
signs of his [God's] existence, but they point both ways and are
therefore ambiguous and so prove nothing . . . the wonders of the
universe do not convince those most conversant with the wonders, the scientists themselves."

Why isn't the Argument from Design more convincing? Percy
is right: nature gives off mixed signals. I left Alaska with sentiments
of worship and admiration; the polar bears' prey probably has a different perspective. And I might have been less anxious to write a
hymn had I pondered instead the design of the Alaskan mosquito
or the Cecidomyian gall midge (whose young hatch inside their
mother and literally eat their way out, devouring the mother as
they go).

Like humanity, the rest of the created world presents a strange
mixture of beauty and horror, of splendid cooperation and sav-
age competition. In the Apostle Paul's words, "We know that the
whole creation has been groaning as in the pains of childbirth

right up to the present time" (Romans 8:22). Nature is our fallen sister, not our mother.

C. S. Lewis used to say that the Christian does not go to nature to learn theology—the message is too garbled—but rather to fill theological words with meaning. "Nature never taught me that there exists a God of glory and of infinite majesty. I had to learn that in other ways. But nature gave the word *glory* a meaning for me. I still do not know where else I could have found one."

I didn't learn much theology on my trip to Alaska. But, wading in a glacial stream dyed red with spawning salmon, and watching a bald eagle pluck a sea bass out of the bay, I did fill a few words with meaning. Words like *joy,* and *awe.*

Just a few miles outside of Anchorage, as I drove along the oddly named inlet Turnagain Arm, I noticed a number of cars pulled off the highway. When Alaskan cars pull over, that usually means animals. Against the slate gray sky, the water of Turnagain Arm appeared to have a slight greenish cast, interrupted by small whitecaps. Soon I saw these were not whitecaps at all, but whales—silvery white beluga whales. A pod was feeding no more than fifty feet offshore. I stood for forty minutes, listening to the rhythmic motion of the sea, following the graceful, ghostly crescents of surfacing whales. The crowd was hushed, even reverent. We passed around binoculars, saying nothing, simply watching. More cars pulled off the road. Dogs chased each other on the shoreline, their owners oblivious. For just that moment, nothing else— dinner reservations, the trip schedule, my life back in the lower forty-eight—mattered.

We were confronted with a scene of quiet beauty and a majesty of scale. We all felt small. We stood together in silence, until the whales moved farther out. And then we climbed the bank together and got in our cars to resume our busy, ordered lives that somehow seemed less urgent. And it wasn't even Sunday.

# Chapter 6

# Reading Genesis in the Wild

After thirteen years in downtown Chicago, my wife and I moved to a remote setting in the Rocky Mountains. I find myself missing the characters in our old neighborhood: the can collector who called himself Tut Uncommon, the mental patient who sat in a coffee shop all day pretending to smoke an unlit cigarette, the eccentric who roamed Clark Street with a sign that read I NEED A WIFE!

In our new location, we see more animals than people. Elk graze on the hill behind our house, woodpeckers pound on the wood siding, and a red fox we've named Foster drops by every evening in search of handouts. The other day Foster sat outside the screen door and listened to an entire segment of Garrison Keillor's radio program as I wallpapered my office. He cocked his head quizzically a few times during the bluegrass music, but all in all seemed to enjoy the show.

Not long after the move, I began reading through the Bible,

starting with Genesis, and soon discovered that the Bible takes on a different tone in new surroundings. I read the creation account during snow season. Mountains gleamed in the morning sunlight, and every ponderosa pine wore a mantle of pure, crystalline white. It was easy to imagine the joy of original creation, a time when, as God later described to Job, "the morning stars sang together and all the angels shouted for joy."

That same week, however, a loud thump interrupted my reading. A small bird, a pine siskin with a notched tail and yellow chevron stripes on each wing, had crashed into the window. It lay stomach-down on a clump of snow, gasping for breath, with bright red drops of blood spilling from its beak. For twenty minutes it lay there, its head nodding as if in drowsiness, until finally it made one last fluttering effort to rise, then dropped its head into the snow and died.

As tragedies go, I had witnessed a minor one. On the noon news I heard of slaughter in the Middle East and bloodshed in Africa. Somehow, though, a single bird's death, enacted just across the windowpane, brought home the gravity of my reading for that day: it captured in miniature the chasmic change between Genesis 2 and 3, between paradise and fallen creation.

The author of Genesis was a master of understatement. A flat report, "Thus the heavens and the earth were completed in all their vast array" (2:1), sums up the stupendous process that brought into being quasars and nebulae, blue whales and dwarf shrimp, penguins and pine siskins. Although presumably written long after the Fall, the first two chapters of Genesis give the merest hints of any tragedy to follow. "They felt no shame," the author says of naked Adam and Eve, a comment that makes sense only to readers acquainted with shame.

Genesis 2 includes another editorial comment as well, one I had never before noticed. In a remarkable scene, God parades the many animals before Adam "to see what he would name them." What a strange new sensation for omnipotence! The Creator of the universe in all its vast array assumes the role of Spectator, waiting "to see" what Adam would do.

We humans have been granted "the dignity of causation," said Blaise Pascal, and the next few chapters of Genesis prove causation to be both dignity and burden. In short order human beings master the basics of family life, agriculture, music, and toolmaking. But they also master the art of murder, fornication, and other deeds drearily characteristic of the species. Before long, God "regrets" his decision to create: "The Lord was grieved that he had made man on the earth, and his heart was filled with pain" (6:6).

Throughout the Old Testament, God seems to alternate between Spectator and Participant. At times, when blood cries out from the ground, when injustice grows intolerable, when evil overruns all constraints, God acts—decisively, even violently. Mountains smoke, the ground yawns open, people die. The New Testament, though, shows the God who selflessly shared the dignity of causation by descending to become its Victim. He who had the right to destroy the world—and had nearly done so once in Noah's day—chose instead to love the world, at any cost.

I sometimes wonder how hard it has been for God *not* to act in history. How must it feel to see the glories of creation—the rain forests, the whales, the elephants—obliterated one by one? How must it feel to see the Jews themselves nearly annihilated? To lose a Son? What is the cost of God's self-restraint?

I had always thought of the Fall in terms of its effect on us humans, namely the penalties outlined in Genesis 3. This time I was struck by its effect on God. The Bible devotes only two chapters to the glories of original creation. All that follows describes the agonizing course of re-creation.

The Bible begins and ends with similar images. In Revelation the garden has been transformed into a city, but a river runs through it, and on each side of the river stands the tree of life. No angel with a flaming sword now guards the tree; its fruit abounds, and even its leaves help "the healing of the nations." Referring back to Genesis 3, Revelation sums up the new reality with these simple words: "No longer will there be any curse."

We live out our days between memory and foretaste. The view out my window—whether it's of the Rocky Mountains or the characters on Clark Street—gives mere glimpses of what God had in mind in Genesis 1 and 2, and of what he has promised in Revelation 21 and 22. I stand in awe at the enormous effort required to restore what has been spoiled. All because God stepped back to see what Adam—what you and I—would do.

# Chapter 7

# Disturbing the Universe

Doubt, for me, tends to come in an overwhelming package, all at once. I don't worry much about nuances of particular doctrines, but every so often I catch myself wondering about the whole grand scheme of faith.

I stand in the futuristic airport in Denver, for example, watching important-looking people in business suits, briefcases clutched to their sides like weapons, pause at an espresso bar before scurrying off to another concourse. *Do any of them ever think about God?* I wonder.

Christians share an odd belief in parallel universes. One universe consists of glass and steel and wool clothes and leather briefcases and the smell of freshly ground coffee. The other consists of angels and sinister spiritual forces and somewhere out there places called Heaven and Hell. We palpably inhabit the material world; it takes faith to consider oneself a citizen of the other, invisible world.

Occasionally the two worlds merge for me, and these rare moments are anchors for my faith. The time I snorkeled on a coral reef and suddenly the flashes of color and abstract design flitting around me became a window to a Creator who exults in life and beauty. The time my wife forgave me for something that did not merit forgiveness—that too became a window, allowing a startling glimpse of divine grace.

I have these moments, but soon toxic fumes from the material world seep in. Sex appeal! Power! Money! Military might! These are what matter most in life, I'm told, not the simpering platitudes of Jesus' teachings in the Sermon on the Mount. For me, living in a fallen world, doubt seems more like *forgetfulness* than disbelief.

Unlike most people, I do not feel much Dickensian nostalgia at Christmastime. The holiday fell just a few days after my father died early in my childhood, and all my memories of the season are darkened by the shadow of that sadness. For this reason, perhaps, I am rarely stirred by the sight of manger scenes and tinseled trees. Yet, more and more, Christmas has enlarged in meaning for me, primarily as an answer to my doubts, an antidote to my forgetfulness.

In Christmas, the two worlds come together. If you read the Bible alongside a Civilization 101 textbook, you will see how seldom that happens. The textbook dwells on the glories of ancient Egypt and the pyramids; the Book of Exodus mentions the names of two Hebrew midwives but neglects to identify the Pharaoh. The textbook honors the contributions from Greece and Rome; the Bible contains a few scant references, mostly negative, and treats great civilizations as mere background static for God's work among the Jews.

Yet on Jesus the two books agree. I switched on my computer this morning and Microsoft Windows flashed the date, implicitly acknowledging what the Gospels and the history book both affirm: whatever you may believe about it, the birth of Jesus was so important that it split history into two parts. Everything that has ever happened on this planet falls into a category of before Christ or after Christ.

In the cold, in the dark, among the wrinkled hills of Bethlehem, God who knows no before or after entered time and space. He who knows no boundaries at all took them on: the shocking confines of a baby's skin, the ominous restraints of mortality. "He is the image of the invisible God, the firstborn over all creation," an apostle would later say; "He is before all things, and in him all things hold together." But the few eyewitnesses on Christmas night saw none of that. They saw an infant struggling to work never-before-used lungs.

Why did Jesus come to earth? Theologians tend to answer that question from the human perspective: He came to show us what God is like, to show us what a human being should be like, to lay down his life as a sacrifice. I cannot help thinking, though, that Incarnation had meaning in other, cosmic ways.

God loves matter. You can read his signature everywhere: rocks that crack open to reveal delicate crystals, the clouds swirling around Venus, the fecundity of the oceans (home to 90 percent of all living things). Clearly, according to Genesis, the act of creation gave God pleasure.

Yet creation also introduced a gulf between God and his subjects, a gulf that can be sensed all through the Old Testament. Moses, David, Jeremiah, and other bold wrestlers with the Almighty flung this accusation to the heavens: "Lord, you don't know what it's like down here!" Job was most blunt: "Do you have eyes of flesh? Do you see as a mortal sees?"

They had a point, a point God himself acknowledged with the decision to visit planet Earth. Choosing words that astonish, the author of Hebrews reflects on Jesus' life as a time when he "learned obedience," "was made perfect," and became a "sympa-thetic" high priest. There is only one way to learn sympathy, as signified by the Greek roots of the word *sym pathos*, "to feel or suffer with."

Of the many reasons for Incarnation, surely one was to answer Job's accusation. *Do you have eyes of flesh?* Yes, indeed.

I, a citizen of the visible world, know well the struggle in-volved in clinging to belief in another, invisible world. Christmas turns the tables and hints at the struggle involved when the Lord of both worlds descends to live by the rules of the one. In Beth-lehem the two worlds came together, realigned; what Jesus went on to accomplish on planet Earth made it possible for God some-day to resolve all disharmonies in both worlds. No wonder a choir of angels broke out in spontaneous song, disturbing not only a few shepherds but the entire universe.

Part Two

✠

Finding

God

on

the

Job

Chapter 8

# They Also Serve Who
# Only Sit and Click

During the years we lived in Chicago, my wife directed a senior citizens' program among the very poor. A typical dinner table conversation in our house went like this:

"How was your day, Janet?"

"Rough. I met a homeless family who'd been living in Lincoln Park and hadn't eaten in three days. After taking care of them I learned that eighty-nine-year-old Peg Martin had died. And then I discovered some gang members had broken into the church van and spray-painted graffiti all over it."

After filling in the details of those adventures, Janet would ask about my day. "Uh, let me think. What did happen today? I stared at a computer screen all day. Oh yeah—just after lunch I found a very good adverb!"

Our daily routines, not to mention our personalities, could hardly differ more. Janet, vivacious, outgoing, gregarious, worked out of an office on Hill Street, the seamy locale made famous by the TV show *Hill Street Blues*. Her days were full of adventure, and full of people: often she served meals to seventy people at a time, and nearly every day she dealt with several dozen clients.

After we moved to Colorado, she began working in a hospice. The average patient admitted there dies within ten days. Janet now came home with stories of families who had differing responses of courage, rage, or despair, but all marked by the passion that grief compels.

Meanwhile, whether in Chicago or Colorado, I sit at home in my basement office staring at a flickering computer screen in search of the perfect word. (So far, computers only process words, they don't compose them.) The main "event" in my day occurs around noon, when the mailman arrives. Occasionally the telephone rings. And once a week or so I may meet someone for lunch. The daily regimen of a writer is not what you'd call glamorous.

You cannot imagine the vicarious thrill I felt when I first came across Philip Roth's description of writing in *The Ghost Writer*:

> I turn sentences around. That's my life. I write a sentence and then I turn it around. Then I look at it and I turn it around again. Then I have lunch. Then I come back in and write another sentence. Then I have tea and turn the new sentence around. Then I read the two sentences over and turn them both around. Then I lie down on my sofa and think. Then I get up and throw them out and start from the beginning.

He has described my life precisely. The vast difference between that sort of life and my wife's used to bother me. Following my usual course of introspection and self-doubt, I would tend to discount my own work and accept blame for not having a more direct impact on people. "Janet puts into practice what I write about," I would say, only half joking, to friends. I left unstated the clear implication that what I did was somehow less valuable, less worthy.

I suppose I encounter my own version of the lonely housewife syndrome: sitting home all day, with such a narrow focus, I have trouble imagining that my daily routine makes much difference to the world or anyone in it. Yes, I get mail from readers, but such letters come long after the act of writing, and the impact they describe is very indirect and vicarious. I observe no immediate results comparable to my wife's, who can watch the actual facial expression change on a hungry person fed, a homeless person sheltered, a grieving person comforted.

In addition, Janet comes home with stories so rich in fascinating detail as to make any writer drool. I remember her visiting a lady named Beulah in the hospital, for example. Beulah was born in 1892 to a wet nurse on a Louisiana plantation. Her mother, freed from slavery long before, had stayed on the plantation, and Beulah grew up playing under the front porch with the rich white children. Later, Beulah got bounced around from the plantation to New Orleans to Tennessee to Chicago. She had lived seventy-two years before Congress ever got around to passing the first civil rights bill!

That night Janet came home full of stories Beulah had dredged up from her childhood days along the levees of the Mississippi River. World War I or II, the Great Depression, the Russian Revolution—you name a major event of the twentieth century and Beulah can resurrect a story about it.

I listen to such stories and think to myself: *If I could have Janet's job, I'd never experience writer's block again.* But then sober reality sets in to self-correct my fantasies. *There are two problems, Philip: First, you'd be terrible at Janet's job, and second, you'd have no time left over to write.* And so the next morning after eating my cereal, I headed downstairs to spend another day making the sound of insect clicks on my computer keyboard.

Over time I have come to see that the very differences between us—in personality, outlook, and daily routine—actually represent a great strength. Janet provides me with a new set of eyes into a world I barely know about. I find challenge there, and stimulation. My own faith is tested as I hear of her attempts to bring hope to the lives of those who have so little. Sometimes, like now, her experiences even edge their way into my writing.

On the other hand, I can offer Janet calmness, reflection, and balance. I try to make our home a haven: a place for her to lick wounds, to gain perspective, to recharge for the next day's battles. (Again, the reverse housewife syndrome—is this not what women offered their career husbands for centuries?)

The New Testament frequently uses the image of the human body to illustrate the church. A body composed of many members with many gifts can accomplish far more than a one-celled organism. Individual cells may suffer an apparent "disadvantage": a human eye cell, for example, never gets to experience touch, or hearing, or anything at all but vision. But because of its specialization, that eye cell can contribute a wholly new level of sight. One-celled amoebas can see enough to galumph away from light, but that's about it.

I have found the same principle applies to marriage as well. I no longer view Janet's work with a sense of competition. Rather, I marvel at the difference in temperament and spiritual gifts that allows her to spend her day dealing with situations that would probably drive me crazy. I have learned to take pride in her work, to see it as a part of my own service to God. By serving her, and offering a listening ear, I can strengthen her and thus help assure that her vital work will continue.

On good days, I remember this principle, pray for Janet, and look for ways to help equip her for her demanding and wonderful work. As for bad days—well, you'll probably find me sitting in front of a computer screen, looking a little cross-eyed, daydreaming of the great novels I could write if I spent my time on Hill Street instead of in my basement.

# Chapter 9

# Letter Bombs

I've always considered it a shame that writing is such a one-way proposition. You know what I'm thinking about but I don't know what you're thinking about—except for the few readers who take the trouble to send in a letter. For this reason, I decided to take a retrospective look at my mailbag from *Christianity Today*, where many of my articles have appeared.

Some letters I receive have no apparent relevance to what I've written and leave me scratching my head. Just the other week I got one that began, "Your article 'Why I Don't Go to a Megachurch' is a perfect example of the state of affairs in America." The writer proceeded in six handwritten pages to trace most of the societal problems in modern America to the fact that "religious men" no longer use the original King James Holy Bible. I'm still looking for a connection to my column.

A reader from Houston sent me clippings of all the local ads for topless dancers, exotic maids, and private lingerie models. This sort of thing *never* appeared in Houston papers before NASA moved to town, he assured me. He also told me that he had personally witnessed two atomic bombs detonated at Bikini Atoll in 1946. Hmm.

In a twelve-page, single-spaced letter, an Englishman described his many allergies and a new program of Optimum Nutrition. Then he detailed the divine revelations he had received by observing clouds and the flight paths of certain birds. I take him very seriously—after all, he lives not far from William Blake's home.

A reader asked me to contribute to a book on touching and hugging. She hoped I could offer "practical suggestions for how men can get comfortable offering hugs or touches of support and love, to each other, maybe even to women. For instance—allow yourself to be hugged first? Find someone who's a good hugger and observe? Touch with hand first? Don't crush? Avoid full body contact? Know which body parts to avoid?" I declined since I did not know the answers to most of these questions. Who said book publishing is a dying industry?

Several people have written me in an attempt to get around the normal magazine channels for evaluating freelance submissions. My favorite sent me a T-shirt with his name on it, and then a decorated cake that read, "Trapped in a bakery. Send work." I shared a piece with the magazine's editor, who mailed him the rejection notice. I think his idea did get special consideration, however.

Sometimes the connection to my writing is all too clear. When I wrote a magazine column titled "Christian McCarthyism," I got several responses from people who felt I had defamed Sen. Joe McCarthy. I now have a file folder devoted to revisionist history of that Cold Warrior. (Once I met Sen. Eugene McCarthy, the 1968 presidential candidate, who has spent his entire political life being confused with the fiery senator from Wisconsin. Not long ago someone stopped him on a street in New York. "Aren't you Senator McCarthy?" the stranger asked. "Why, yes," McCarthy replied. Then came the unexpected question, "Do you still hate communists?")

By far the most mail I have ever received came in response to my 1993 column "Breakfast at the White House." I stopped counting at three hundred letters, perhaps three of which were positive. Readers seemed offended that a Christian would even sit down at the same table with Bill Clinton and Al Gore. Seven writers asked if I would have dined with Adolf Hitler. I was astonished by the vicious tone of some of these letters, until I finally figured out that the writers were projecting onto me the anger they really felt toward Bill Clinton. I'd hate to read his mail.

One reader told me that God had personally revealed to him that a high school student could do a better job of running the country than Bill Clinton and that God was thinking about letting "Mr. Satin not satan take him out in death if he didn't improve." He also disclosed to me some important clues to the identity of the Antichrist and enclosed a magic sponge which, when saturated with water, would reveal a telephone number where I could get help for my spiritual problems.

My all-time favorite letter came from a reader in Seattle. He began with a few jokes about Seventh-day Adventists, and then got down to serious business. Just as C. S. Lewis had appeared to writer J. B. Phillips after his death, this reader had received a supernatural visit from J. B. Phillips. He had also met the composers Handel and Dvořák, and had once played second violin in an orchestra conducted by Haydn. Handel, he reported, is no longer blind but wears thick glasses that allow him to drive a car, and currently directs a choir at a Presbyterian church that has only thirty-three members. Dvořák lives in the town of Edmonds, Washington.

With absolute assurance, this reader promised that if I moved to Seattle within thirty days, he would arrange a personal meeting with C. S. Lewis. That was about the time I moved to Colorado, and I asked the post office from then on to forward all my business mail to the magazine's office in Illinois.

Chapter 10

# The Never-Never Land
# of Religious Media

Because I spend so much of my life alone in a basement office, when I do emerge outdoors I sometimes feel like a mole blinking in the light. Never was this more true than when I agreed to do an author's media tour. For several weeks I visited television and radio stations as part of a campaign to introduce my book *Disappointment with God*.

I knew I was in trouble the very first day, in Dallas, when a radio station booked me on a talk show with a Christian comedian. An expert at mouth sounds and hand sounds, he could precisely duplicate the noises made by barnyard animals, race cars, and train wrecks. Between the two of us, we covered the bases: he could do a perfect imitation of a jet plane taking off, and I could try to explain why God allows airplanes to crash. Why did I feel like a character in an absurdist play?

From there I drove to a Baptist television station to field phone calls on a televised counseling show. The program was exceptionally well run, but not without its strange aspects. The topic "Disappointment with God" attracted callers who had wrenching personal stories: child abuse, alcoholism, cancer, AIDS, you name it. As these callers spilled out their traumas over staticky phone lines, I could only stare into a camera and nod sympathetically. Meanwhile in my peripheral vision, the show's producers were running around holding up large placards: "This man's a crank. Get him off the air!" and "Wind it up fast! Thirty seconds to commercial break!" In Los Angeles, I spent three hours and fifty minutes in helpless agitation on a gridlocked freeway, listening to the radio program I was supposed to be on. "We know you're out there on the freeway, Philip," the gracious host said over the air. "Just drive carefully. Don't worry." I did drive carefully—could I do otherwise at five miles per hour? I also worried, and with good reason: I never made it to the show.

In San Francisco, I appeared on the same program with a former Las Vegas showgirl who was now spearheading an effort to build a sixty-story prayer tower in the shape of a cross in every major U.S. city. She had been converted through a near-death experience on the operating table. "My career was suffering so I had to get my *bustes* enlarged again," she said. While she lay anesthetized, an angel escorted her to Hell, where she saw an eighteen-wheeler composed entirely of human flesh—"Even the mud flaps were made of flesh!"—dumping America's teenagers into a molten lake. Now I ask you, how can any work of popular theology compete on a program that has stories like that?

My media tour ended at Heritage USA, the vestigial organization that survived the fall of Jim and Tammy Faye Bakker. I had visited the grounds twice before, once in the Bakkers' heyday and once during the more somber reign of Jerry Falwell. The mood this time was palpably different. The central cluster of Disneylandish buildings glowed out of the darkness like Las Vegas after a neutron bomb. There were many buildings in this phantom city, but no people. All exuberance was gone. Condominiums were shuttered, construction cranes stood idle, the water slide was dry. I went on an eerie jog along the Walk of Faith, marked with bronze plaques inscribed with slogans of prosperity and faith. The television ministry, however, was still limping along, operated by a skeleton crew under the supervision of a bankruptcy court.

Thinking back on my previous visits, I noticed that the biggest change was in the staff members themselves. Many had been hired by the Bakkers, whom they had lionized, but had gradually become disillusioned by the shocking revelations of wrongdoing. The remnant who stayed on did so because they truly believed in the ministry. They seemed humble, genuine, broken. They seemed Christian.

After three weeks of such experiences in the never-never land of religious media, I came up with some subjective, unscientific observations:

1. Christian television stations hire a disproportionate number of beautiful women who wear their hair and their dresses long. Most of these have Southern accents.
2. At least half the time, the interview host first sets eyes on a guest author's book five minutes before the interview program.
3. Charismatic stations can't figure out why anyone would want to write a book on disappointment with God.
4. Of the programs I visited, those run by Southern Baptists and Seventh-day Adventists were the best organized, with their hosts most eager for a conversation of substance. (But try to get a good cup of coffee at a Seventh-day Adventist studio!)
5. On secular stations, callers were obsessed with one question: "How can a loving God permit so much suffering?" On Christian stations, the callers were

obsessed with the opposite: "Yes, God directly causes suffering, and here's why. . . ."

It took a while for me to adjust to the built-in *artificiality* of the media. In normal life you determine how you're relating to the rest of the world by attending to such clues as body language and eye contact. If you're speaking before a group and everyone looks closed-eyed and slack-jawed, you surmise you're not communicating well. But the television and radio audience, of course, remains invisible. Is anyone paying attention? You can't tell. In the television studio itself, the hosts/hostesses bother to act interested in what you're saying only when the camera angle includes them. Otherwise, they may be studying the next question, whispering to the producer, primping in a mirror, straightening a tie.

The call-in format, increasingly popular, introduces a new level of artificiality. I learned quickly why politicians rely on "sound bites." The message must adapt to the medium, not vice versa. When a woman called in, sobbing, to tell me her lifelong story of unrelieved tragedy, I could hardly say, "I'm sorry, but there's not a thing I could tell you in the next ninety seconds to fix a deep-rooted problem like that." Instead, I searched for a capsule summary, some insight that even in abbreviated form might offer a new perspective or simply give hope. Ninety seconds later, we cut to a commercial and I never heard from the woman again.

Sometimes the callers would preface their stories with the statement, "I've never told this to anyone before." It was a frightening disclosure, one that gets to the heart of the central strength—and weakness—of religious broadcasting: some of these people had a closer relationship with their television sets than with any living human being.

## Chapter 11

# The Power of Writing

In a scene from the movie *Black Robe*, a Jesuit missionary tries to persuade a Huron chief to let him teach the tribe to read and write. The chief sees no benefit to this practice of scratching marks on paper until the Jesuit gives him a demonstration. "Tell me something I do not know," he says. The chief thinks for a moment and replies, "My woman's mother died in snow last winter."

The Jesuit writes a sentence and walks a few yards over to his colleague, who glances at it and then says to the chief, "Your mother-in-law died in a snowstorm?" The chief jumps back in alarm. He has just encountered the magical power of writing, which allows knowledge to leap across space and travel in silence through symbols.

Augustine's *Confessions* gives a wonderful glimpse of Saint Ambrose, who had mastered the art of reading silently, without moving his lips. Augustine and his friends would gather to watch this feat, amazed that Ambrose could comprehend and retain the unpronounced words, as if by telepathy. Until the thirteenth century, in fact, very few people could read in such a novel way. (Mastery of such a practice, interestingly, led to a surge in private prayer: until then believers viewed both prayer and reading as group activities.)

I once read a long and at times tedious study called *The History and Power of Writing*, by Henri-Jean Martin, which sets out many examples of writing's impact on the world. Most of history has viewed writing as a supplement to the more reliable medium of oral communication. Scholars recorded epic poems or lists of facts as an aid to memory, but rarely used writing to communicate new ideas. For the epic poets, writing proved entirely too constraining: no longer could they play to the audience by adding embellishment to the recitations. Indeed, stripped of inflection and facial expression, detached from the sensory surroundings of the campfire or banquet hall, incapable of dialogue, writing seemed a thin, frail medium.

The church has had a love/hate relationship with writing, even though it was invented as a way to record truths about the sacred. (Druids resisted writing for this reason—they didn't want their secrets to get out.) Clerics led the way in bringing literacy to Europe, and during the Dark Ages monasteries preserved the classics while society crumbled around them.

Yet through its book-burnings, censorship, and persecution of authors, the church also tried to control writing. Such controls fell apart during the Protestant Reformation, which happened to coincide with the invention of the printing press. Reformers saw writing as a freedom-enhancing medium. By translating the Bible and other books into vernacular language and distributing them widely, they could free doctrine from the thought police of the church hierarchy. Soon, of course, Protestant thought police emerged too, but with less effect: the word had been irretrievably set free.

Reading Henri-Jean Martin's book on the history of writing, I could not help reflecting on my own pilgrimage. I grew up in a Southern fundamentalist church that taught blatant racism, apocalyptic fear of communism, and America-first patriotism. Christian doctrine was dished out in a "believe and don't ask questions" style, laced with fervid emotionalism.

For me, reading opened a chink of light that became a window to another world. I remember the impact of a mild book like *To Kill a Mockingbird*, which called into question the apartheid assumptions of my friends and neighbors. Later, reading books like *Black Like Me, The Autobiography of Malcolm X*, and Martin Luther King's *Letter from Birmingham City Jail*, I felt my whole world shatter. Like the startled Huron chief, I too experienced the power that allowed one human mind to penetrate another with no intermediary but a piece of flattened wood pulp.

I especially came to value the freedom-enhancing aspect of writing. Speakers in the churches I attended could RAISE THEIR VOICES! and play emotions like musical instruments. But alone in my room, voting with every turn of the page, I met other representatives of the Kingdom—Saint Augustine, C. S. Lewis, G. K. Chesterton—whose calmer voices leapt across time to convince me that somewhere Christians lived who knew grace as well as law, love as well as judgment, reason as well as passion.

I became a writer, I believe, because of my own experience of the power of words. I saw that spoiled words, their original meaning wrung out, could be reclaimed. I saw that writing could penetrate into the crevices, bringing spiritual oxygen to people trapped in airtight boxes. I saw that when God conveyed to us the essence of his self-expression, God called it the Word. And the Word comes in the most freedom-enhancing way imaginable.

I feel both proud and ashamed of my profession. We have at times used words like clubs, not levers. We have used words to enslave, not liberate. Even so, somehow the written word has endured. I think of Irish monks laboring for weeks, even months, over single letters of illuminated manuscripts, keeping the word alive in an age when few people could read, or cared to. I think of faithful writers like Solzhenitsyn, who relied on the samizdat press to distribute hand-typed sheaves of witness from hand to hand.

We may be entering a different kind of Dark Ages, a time when the Devil owns the airwaves and when words seem gray and dull compared to the dazzle of virtual reality and multimedia DVDs. I have hope, though. Despite the waves of hysteria and authoritarianism in church history, words of truth have survived and emerged later as living forces to change individuals and entire cultures. I have experienced their power. I pray that the church, in increasingly oppressive times, will remember that words have their greatest impact when they enhance freedom, when they liberate.

# Chapter 12

# God at Large

A friend of mine recently returned from a visit to Asian countries where Christians are experiencing persecution. Christians in Malaysia told him, "We're so blessed, because in Indonesia they're killing Christians, but here we just have to put up with discrimination and restrictions on our activities." In Indonesia, where Christians are indeed dying for their faith, they told him, "We're very blessed, because in Malaysia they can't freely publish the gospel. Here, we still can." The church in Indonesia values the power of words.

My job as a writer affords me the opportunity to visit a variety of countries, including some that oppress Christians. I have noticed a striking difference in the wording of prayers. When difficulties come, Christians in affluent countries tend to pray, "Lord, take this trial away from us!" I have heard persecuted Christians and some who live in very poor countries pray instead, "Lord, give us the strength to bear this trial."

Curious, I asked an old-time missionary, who has made a dozen trips to visit unregistered house churches in China, if Christians there prayed for a change in restrictive government policies. He replied that not once had he heard a Chinese Christian pray for relief. "They just assume they'll face opposition," he said. "They can't imagine anything else." He then gave some examples of the opposition.

One pastor had served a term of twenty-two years at hard labor for holding unauthorized church meetings. When he emerged from prison and returned to church, he announced that he had kept a daily count on his dangerous job, and had coupled together 1 million railroad cars without an injury. "God answered your prayers for my safety!" he rejoiced. Working near the Russian border without warm clothing, he had also avoided serious illness all that time.

Another imprisoned pastor heard that his wife was going blind. Desperate, he reported to the warden that he was renouncing his faith. He was released, but soon felt so guilty that he again turned himself in to the police. He spent the next thirty years in prison.

One year I visited Brazil and the Philippines, two relatively poor countries where the church is experiencing explosive growth. Local groups had invited me to bring encouragement to the church, but I ended up as the one encouraged. In both places, when people receive Christian literature on the street, they stop and read it; when invited to a Christian meeting, they actually go. Even the media lacks a veneer of cynicism. Politicians and pop music stars get converted and talk openly about their faith; evangelicals write faith-building columns in the daily newspaper. One church I addressed in Manila holds five services on Sunday; the first, which meets at 5 A.M., has two thousand in attendance.

Such nations are in a "honeymoon" phase with Christianity.

The gospel still sounds like good news. I met Brazilians who welcome homeless street urchins into their families and who bring food to prisoners—voluntarily, not under anyone's organized program. Poor villages that have never heard terms like "social justice" or "liberation theology" find their economic status rising as the converted breadwinners stop drinking, show up for work on time, and start acting like responsible citizens.

Other nations have settled into a "divorced" phase. That same year I also visited Denmark, a nation that vies with the Czech Republic as having the lowest rate of church attendance. Church steeples pierce the gray skies, but only tourists bother to go inside. No one could tell me a single place where I might find anything related to Denmark's most famous Christian thinker, Søren Kierkegaard. In the national museum, a placard explained that the cross, formerly the religious symbol of Denmark, is now regarded as a cultural relic.

Some nations are in a mature marriage phase. In the United States, nearly half of us attend church on a given Sunday, and Christians have a visible presence on university campuses and in every major profession. Politicians running for office compete with each other in appealing to the religious constituency. Both church and parachurch, though, sometimes seem to operate more like an industry than a living organism. We hire others to take care of the orphans and visit the prisoners; we pay professionals to lead the worship. To return from a church in Brazil to one in the U.S. is like moving from a down-home county fair, where everyone gets to pet the cows and chase the pigs, to Disney World's wild animal park, where you pay a fee to watch the beasts (some of which are mechanical) from behind a barrier.

According to some estimates, Christians in developed Western countries now represent only 37 percent of believers worldwide. As I travel and also read church history, I have observed a pattern, a strange historical phenomenon of God "moving" geographically from place to place: from the Middle East to Europe to North

America to the developing world. My theory is this: God goes where he's wanted.

That's a scary thought in a country like the United States, home to a robust economy and five hundred satellite TV channels for diversion and entertainment, not to mention Disney World.

Part Three

✠

Finding

God

in

the

Rubble

## Chapter 13

# Grace at Ground Zero

The phones started ringing at our house on September 11, the day of the attack. I got calls from England, Holland, and Australia as well as from U.S. media. "You've written about the problem of pain. What do you have to say about the tragedy?"

In truth, I had nothing to say. The facts were so overpowering, so incomprehensible, that I was stunned into silence. Anything I could think of saying—Horrible . . . Don't blame God . . . We've seen the face of evil . . . —sounded like a jejune cliché. In every case I declined to respond. Like most Americans, I felt unbearably helpless, and wounded, and deeply sad.

On Wednesday, the day after the attacks, it dawned on me that I had already written much of what I believe about the problem of pain. I wrote *Where Is God When It Hurts?* in 1977, as a twenty-eight-year-old who had no right to tackle questions of theodicy—and also no ability to resist, for there is no more urgent question facing those of us who identify ourselves as Christian. In 1990, I revised the book, adding about a hundred pages and the perspective of middle age.

That night I e-mailed a proposal to my publisher, Zondervan, suggesting that we find a way to get that book out as cheaply as possible to as many people as possible. The book title was, after all, the question everyone in America was asking then. I could forgo all royalties, and they could forgo all profit, as our contribution to a grieving nation. They jumped on the idea with amazing speed. Already they had been discussing various "instant books." Instead they decided to put their full resources into getting *Where Is God?* into as many hands as possible. They called the next morning (Thursday, two days after the tragedy) saying they were mobilizing for a special edition.

By Friday, Zondervan had 500,000 orders for a one-time-only edition with all proceeds directed to the victims' fund. In short, they sold as many copies in twenty-four hours as they had sold in the previous twenty-four years. Wal-Mart ordered 125,000; airport bookstores ordered scores of thousands. It seems that retailers, too, felt helpless and grasped at a chance to offer a book that might give perspective on questions their customers were consumed with. Against all odds, the publisher found available printing press time, and paper, and by Saturday, four days after the World Trade Center attack, copies were being printed.

The flurry of activity, occurring at such speed with almost instantaneous results, made me feel considerably less helpless. I soon received my first response from a reader of the special edition. Her choir director had driven from Florida to North Carolina to be by the side of a family member undergoing surgery. He had planned to fly, but airplane cancellations after September 11 forced him to drive. He never made it; an auto accident killed him. Standing in a bookstore, weeping, this woman had noticed my book on pain and bought it—one of many who suffered "collateral damage" from the terrorist acts.

One day I turned on my computer to find an extraordinary journal e-mailed from Gordon MacDonald, a pastor and author who is also a friend. Gordon, who had once served a church in Manhattan, cleared his schedule when he first heard about the attacks and volunteered as a chaplain with the Salvation Army. Each night, after a grueling day near Ground Zero, he recorded the sights and sounds and, yes, the smells he and his wife Gail had encountered that day.

I called Gordon to tell him how deeply his journal had affected me, and when he learned I would soon spend a day in New York City on a book tour, he insisted that I visit Ground Zero and see for myself. Five minutes later he called back to say he had made the arrangements with top officials at the Salvation Army.

Salvation Army personnel, bless them, are not the most publicity-savvy people in the world. Gordon MacDonald told me that certain other groups always made sure media interviews were conducted with their van and its prominent logo in the background, for the TV cameras. Such a thought would never occur to an organization with a name like "Salvation Army."

Whenever I speak to Salvation Army groups, I joke that if someone held a contest for the most oxymoronic name for an organization, theirs would surely win. Imagine slamming together the musty theological word "salvation" and the military word "army." Yet, by my reckoning, that army is now the third-largest standing army in the world. With military discipline and commitment, they join together to bring grace and healing to a desperately needy world.

I have a soft spot in my heart for the Salvation Army because my great-grandfather got converted to Christ away from a life of alcoholism at a Philadelphia rescue mission run by the Salvation Army. He attended the church service because he wanted a bowl of soup, and responded to the invitation to go forward simply out of politeness. He was the most surprised man in Philadelphia when the prayer actually worked. After that night he never drank another drop. He spent the rest of his life apologizing to his children, now grown, who had been victims of his violent alcoholic rages.

I have read a little of the history of the Army, and I love William Booth's decision to form a church among the "trophies of grace," the down-and-out in East London, when no traditional churches would accept them. Booth understood like few people in history the truth that God's grace, like water, flows to the lowest part. Wearing uniforms that haven't changed much in a century, Booth's soldiers now roll up their sleeves and serve others at the most basic human level.

The Salvation Army may have military discipline and commitment, though perhaps not the same precision. On a very tight time schedule, I had arranged to take a tour of Ground Zero along with the visiting commissioner of Australia, but we sat around for two hours before S.A. personnel figured out the logistics and the paperwork required to get us through security checkpoints. That "wasted time" gave me an opportunity to visit with some of the Salvationists who had been serving at Ground Zero.

While sitting around sipping coffee, I met Maj. Carl Ruthberg, who was normally stationed at Times Square. After the tragedy he worked at the medical examiner's office, the place where they brought bodies and body parts to be identified. The morgue was equipped with high-tech refrigerator trucks lined with steel shelving and body bags stacked by the thousands. Two weeks after the event, only 5 percent of the bodies had been found. One group was found intact, holding hands, but they were a rarity. The rest lay buried under tons of rubble or they had simply vaporized in the heat.

The Jewish rabbi assigned to the morgue said his tradition did not prepare him for the task. Jews have a practice of staying with a body from death to burial, which is why they arrange funerals within twenty-four hours. At Ground Zero, there were few bodies to stay with. When I visited, a full two weeks had passed with several thousand bodies still missing.

Major Ruthberg told me of the rescue dogs who got so discouraged that their handlers had to play games with them to keep up their interest; they would hide under blankets to let the dogs "find" them. The dogs searched all day and found maybe a piece of clothing or an elbow or scrap of skin. They cut their paws on the sharp edges of steel and whined in frustration because, like the human rescuers, they had so little to show for their efforts.

He also told of what happened when evidence of a fireman or policeman was found—maybe a badge, or chunk of clothing, or piece of a boot. Machinery was turned off, Ground Zero grew silent, and all firemen on the scene formed two lines and stood at attention. The rescuers who retrieved the clothing or body part then walked in silence between the lines of saluting firemen to the morgue. There they wrapped the body bag in an American flag and placed it in an ambulance, which drove through another line of saluting firemen accompanied by a motorcycle escort, lights flashing but still in silence.

"I am working side by side with heroes," the major said. "And I tell you, they love God. They may be hard-nosed New York detectives, or FBI officers, but at the morgue the softness comes out. I feel privileged to be there, and to offer just a calming word, a touch. We have so few survival stories down here, but we tell them over and over. I keep reminding the guys of all the thousands of people who escaped, partly through their efforts, after the blasts. We lost several thousand, but it could have been ten times that number. We've got to have that balance, a reminder that some did survive."

Gordon MacDonald tells of visiting a former cocktail lounge near Ground Zero, all its windows broken so that you could see the bar inside, and behind it all the liquor bottles and the drinking glasses as they'd been lined up the day of the explosion. Tables and chairs were overturned, and thick dust and pulverized concrete covered every surface. On the mirror above the bar someone had written the name and number of his fire brigade and then added the words, "Others run out; we run in!"

I came to believe that motto captures the mission of the Salvation Army itself. Salvationists like Major Ruthberg and the others I met have no unusual skills or training to distinguish them from many other citizens. They have, though, a firm commitment to dash in, and remain in, places where the natural instinct would be to flee. They soldier on.

As a journalist, I sometimes divide the people I have interviewed into "stars" and "servants." The stars are the people we put on the covers of our magazines and fawn over: beauties, politicians, the wealthy, sports heroes. We lavish attention on them even though, as I have found, many of them live tortured lives I would never want to emulate. I have also interviewed servants, who take literally Jesus' oft-repeated statement that we find our lives by giving them away in service to others. These are the people who brought me back to faith. And in the Salvation Army, I find an entire organization mobilized to put that spirit of service into action.

I have met few "stars" in the Salvation Army. Yes, they have chaplains and substance-abuse counselors and administrators with good skills and excellent training. Yet by belief and by culture, the Salvation Army does not shine a spotlight on these people. Like good soldiers, each person has a job to perform, and the mission always remains the focus, not the people who accomplish that mission.

My guide at Ground Zero was Lt. Col. Damon Rader, brother of Gen. Paul Rader. There are four Rader brothers, all of whom served as top officers in the S.A.: one as a doctor, another as a general, another as a theologian, and another, Damon, as a missionary to Zambia.

Here is how Gordon MacDonald described Damon Rader in his journal:

> Colonel Damon Rader, our partner, is more and more
> a delight to us each day. When we get into the car to drive
> into the city, he grips the steering wheel and begins to
> mutter a prayer under his breath. "The Lord is our refuge
> and strength—help us, dear God, keep us, strengthen us . . .
> make us a blessing . . . oh, God help those men and
> women." And as we drive, I'll hear him from time to time
> just slip into an utterance of prayer. He really does walk in
> and out of God's presence. And there is nothing put on
> about it. He has given his entire life to the Army, lost his
> wife nine years ago and mourns her passing greatly. He has
> been in Zambia since 1959 and plans to return—even
> though retired—there in January "as soon as my
> replacement over there has got his feet on the ground and
> feels confident that he's in full charge." He is really
> indefatigable. I am 62 and have the strength to pull these
> 10–12 hour days, but I watch him closely to see if he's
> keeping up. And he is! He has a cheering, prayerful word
> for everyone. Old William and Catherine Booth would
> have been proud of Damon; he's vintage Army. I love the
> toughness of his Christianity.

I too came to appreciate the cheerful toughness of the Army. I saw more smiles and heard more casual joking in the Salvation Army center than I would see and hear all the rest of the day. These soldiers worked in the morgue and served on the front lines in circumstances that caused tough firemen and police officers to break down. Over the years, though, they had developed an inner strength based on discipline, on community, and above all on a clear vision of whom they were serving. The Salvation Army may have a hierarchy of command, but every soldier knows he or she is performing for an audience of One. As one told me, Salvationists serve in order to earn the ultimate accolade from God himself: "Well done, thy good and faithful servant."

When we finally did get the clearance to drive through the checkpoints, the street was lined with New Yorkers—*New Yorkers!*—waving banners with simple messages. "We love you. You're our heroes. God bless you. Thank you." Gordon MacDonald said that in the early days, crowds ten deep lined these streets at midnight, cheering every rescue vehicle that rolled by. The workers were running on that support as their vehicles ran on fuel. They had so little good news in a day. They faced a mountainously depressing task of removing tons and tons of twisted steel, compacted dirt, smashed equipment, broken glass. But every time they drove past the barricades, they faced a line of fans cheering them on, like the tunnel of cheerleaders that football players run through, reminding them that an entire nation appreciated their service. In a Salvation Army van with lights flashing, we attracted some of the loudest cheers of all.

Moises Serrano, the Salvation Army officer leading us, was incident director for the city. He had been on the job barely a month when the planes hit. He worked thirty-six straight hours and slept four, forty hours and slept six, forty more hours and slept six. Then he took a day off. His assistant had an emotional breakdown early on, in the same van I was riding in, and may never recover.

Many of the Salvationists I met hailed from Florida, the hurricane crews who keep fully stocked canteens and trucks full of basic supplies to send to cities and towns devastated by hurricanes. When the Manhattan buildings fell, they mobilized all those trucks and drove them to New York.

The crew director told me, "To tell you the truth, I came up here expecting to deal with Yankees, if you know what I mean. Instead, it's all smiles and 'Thank you.'"

Salvation Army representatives would certainly counsel you and pray with you if you wanted, and at Ground Zero the Salvationists in the shiny red "Chaplain" jackets were sought after for just that reason. Mainly, though, they were there to assist with more basic human needs: to wash out eyes stinging from smoke and provide Blistex for parched lips, and foot inserts for boots walking across hot metal. They operated hydration stations and snack canteens. They offered a place to rest and freshly cooked chicken courtesy of Tyson's. The day I arrived, they distributed 1,500 phone cards for the workers to use in calling home. Every day they served 7,500 meals. They offered an oasis of compassion in a wilderness of rubble.

We passed through five checkpoints, the last one, known as the Red Zone, manned by American soldiers in army fatigues. "Things have tightened up here," our Salvationist guide shouted over the roar of machinery and generators. "New York's finest take training in public relations. The U.S. Army doesn't." As we approached Ground Zero, we traded our van for an open golf-cart-like vehicle. Soldiers wearing gas masks sprayed water and disinfectant on the tires—water to combat asbestos, disinfectant to fight the germs that flourish around a scene of death. They scrutinized each person's ID and waved us through.

I had studied the maps in newspapers, but no two-dimensional representation could capture the scale of destruction. For about eight square blocks buildings were deserted, their windows broken, jagged pieces of steel jutting out from floors high above the street. Thousands of offices equipped with faxes, phones, and computers sat vacant, coated in debris. On September 11, people were sitting there punching keys, making phone calls, grabbing a cup of coffee to start the day, and suddenly it must have seemed like the world was coming to an end.

The chaplains had warned me about the stench of death, but I mainly smelled the acrid aroma of rubble that had already been burning for two weeks. The air was clear. I was surprised that the streets and sidewalks were clean, not coated with dust. The constant spraying, aided by a couple of rainstorms, had had an effect.

I studied the faces of the workers, uniformly grim. I didn't see a single smile at Ground Zero. How could you smile in such a place? It had nothing to offer but death and destruction, a monument to the worst that human beings can do to each other.

I saw three booths set up in a vacant building across from the WTC site: Police Officers for Christ, Firemen for Christ, and Sanitation Workers for Christ (that last one is a charity I'd like to support). Salvation Army chaplains had told me that police and firemen had asked for two prayer services a day, conducted at the site. The Red Cross, a nonsectarian organization, had asked if the Salvationists would mind staffing it. "Are you kidding? That's what we're here for!"


As I talked to media people about the special edition of *Where Is God When It Hurts?*, inevitably the interviewer would turn the question back on me. "Well, where is God at a time like this?" Sometimes I countered some of the harmful things other Christian spokesmen had said about the attacks being God's judgment on America, bringing guilt and confusion to a time that begged for comfort and grace. I talked of Jesus' response to tragedies, especially in Luke 13. And then I would usually tell of a man who came up to me once and said, "Sorry, I don't have time to read your book. Can you just answer that question for me in a sentence or two?"

Taken aback, I thought for a moment and said, "I guess the answer to that question is another question. Where is the church when it hurts? If the church is doing its job—binding wounds, comforting the grieving, offering food to the hungry—I don't think people will wonder so much where God is when it hurts. They'll know where God is: in the presence of God's people on earth."

Gordon MacDonald had written this in his journal:

And more than once I asked myself—as everyone asks—*is God here?* And I decided that He is closer to this place than any other place I've ever visited. The strange irony is that, amidst this absolute catastrophe of unspeakable proportions, there is a beauty in the way human beings are acting that defies the imagination. Everyone—underscore, everyone— is everyone else's brother or sister. There are no strangers among the thousands at the work site. Everyone talks; everyone cooperates; everyone does the next thing that has to be done. No job is too small, too humble, or, on the other hand, too large. Tears ran freely, affection was exchanged openly, exhaustion was defied. We all stopped caring about ourselves. The words "it's not about me" were never more true.

No church service; no church sanctuary; no religiously inspiring service has spoken so deeply into my soul and witnessed to the presence of God as those hours last night at the crash site.

In all my years of Christian ministry, I never felt more alive than I felt last night. The only other time I can remember a similar feeling was the week that Gail & I worked on a Habitat for Humanity project in Hungary. As much as I love preaching the Bible and all the other things that I have been privileged to do over the years, being on that street, giving cold water to workmen, praying and weeping with them, listening to their stories was the closest I have ever felt to God. Even though it sounds melodramatic, I kept finding myself saying, "This is the place where Jesus most wants to be."

President Bush quoting Psalm 23 in the National Cathedral, the bagpiper by St. Paul's piping "Amazing Grace" over and over, the sanitation workers stopping by their makeshift chapel, the Salvation Army workers dispensing grace, the chaplains comforting the grieving loved ones—thanks to them, we know where God is when it hurts.

# Chapter 14

# A Muslim Seeker

e have grown used to the violent deeds of radical Islamists. They murder Baptist missionaries in Iraq, blow up trains in Spain, bomb a nightclub in Bali, target American soldiers in Afghanistan, take hostages in the Philippines, plot acts of terror around the world. Until the World Trade Center attacks, though, the United States was innocent of such strikes on its soil. The events of that day slammed into our national consciousness like a meteor from outer space.

All my work ceased the morning of September 11, 2001. Like most Americans, I sat glued to the television watching the incredible events unfold. First reports speculated that as many as fifty thousand people had died in the attacks, a figure that proved mercifully high.

The next day I still could not work. I sat at my desk watching a portable television, still trying to absorb the news. And then the fax machine lurched into motion, spitting out a letter from a person I've never met, a Pakistani living in the U.S. It gives personal, individual focus to a conflict normally discussed in global terms, and also poses an important

*challenge to the church. For me, everything going on in the world took on*
*a different slant because of this letter.*

September 12, 2001

Dear Mr. Yancey,

Considering the terrible tragedy that happened yesterday in
this nation, I don't know whether this is the appropriate
time to write about something personal. But perhaps
because of what happened I think I should write this letter,
because I am firmly convinced now that evil does exist in
this world. And for the past few months, I have been on my
own spiritual search for the God of love and goodness. I
know you must be an extremely busy person and I am just
an ordinary guy, but I hope you can get the time to read
this letter.

Why I am writing to you? Because after reading your
books, I get this feeling that you are a person of a very kind
heart and someone who really does have a true and good
idea what Christian faith is really all about (which is of
course not legalism).

Growing up in Pakistan, I was a moderately religious
Muslim, by no stretch of imagination a strict Muslim at all. I
always had a deep dislike and mistrust of the Islamic
establishment there because of their hypocrisy and
fanaticism. But I always had a very good view of the Islamic
faith itself (though I never had done any detailed study of
the faith and knew only what I was told in the school
textbooks and in the mosque).

I came to the U.S. in 1999 as a graduate student. During
the past few months, some of the events in my life caused
me to think about God. A friend of mine had a brain tumor
and that caused me an immense amount of pain and sent me

searching for the answer "why." So I started doing some research into my religion. I read some books about the prophet Muhammad and the Islamic faith by some Western scholars (some seemed biased but some did not seem to have any axe to grind). I was really shocked to learn a lot of things about my religion which I never knew were part of it. I had a very ideal image of my religion and that ideal image got totally shattered. I felt and still feel betrayed and hurt. In a closed society like Pakistan, one can't really have any unbiased view of the Islamic faith, as any sort of criticism of Islam is punishable by death according to the law. And certainly I had never even given a thought about the Christian faith there in Pakistan, even though there is a lot in common between Islam and Christianity.

As I found out all these not-so-agreeable things about the Islamic faith, I found myself drawn toward the Christian faith for no apparent reason (since no one ever tried to talk to me about it or convince me in any way). And that is what is kind of baffling, that this interest in Christianity really came out of nowhere. So I tried to read a little bit about it but soon realized I had to talk to someone. I did not know any churches or anything. So I just called and met with a local Baptist pastor. Over the past few months, I met with him at regular intervals and every time I asked him a lot of questions. Each time he would give me some books to read, but I have also read a lot of other books too. I have read people like Hans Küng (the German theologian), C. S. Lewis, Peter Kreeft, Ravi Zacharias, Billy Graham, Max Lucado, Lee Strobel, and others. As I got to know more about the Christian faith I got to realize that the Christian faith is really not that simple as some people think it is.

For a Muslim person to be that much interested in the Christian faith is something really unthinkable. You see, in a culture like Pakistan's, religion is not just a personal thing. It is part of everything, a very integral part of the family and social life. No one ever even imagines to give up their Islamic faith; it is simply unthinkable. So as I was doing all this research into Christianity, I just did not have the courage to tell my family what I was up to. I started avoiding talking to my two sisters and to my parents in Pakistan. But eventually I did give them some hint and gradually told them everything I was doing. And my family, especially my mom, has been extremely hurt. And that is why I have been going through so much pain, because I really really love my family so much and I don't want to hurt anyone.

And yet there is so much I know about Islam which I just can't seem to accept in my heart. I don't have a religion anymore, I have totally lost it. I do believe in God but I don't think I can say that I am a Muslim anymore in my heart. And that has been so devastating to my mom especially. My parents are visiting the U.S. these days and I have had several religious discussions with them. We have talked about issues like the concept of salvation in Islam (which is through deeds) and that of Christianity. They find quite ridiculous the concept of a savior and one person dying for everyone's sins—that all you have to do is to believe in the savior, and that works don't give you salvation. To be honest, I find this concept a little strange too.

They just find it so strange when I say to them that there really are no categories of sin, that sin is a sin, that there is no major or minor sin, that according to Jesus, anger is as bad as murder. They quite naturally ask me, *Are you crazy or something to be saying something like that?* We have talked about the supposed inaccuracy and corruption of the Bible. Islam does believe in the virgin birth of Jesus but it says that he was a prophet of God and no more. Also, that he was lifted up by God and was not crucified—the Jews only thought that they crucified him. Islam even believes in the second coming of Jesus.

I have found myself defending the Christian beliefs against my family. I argue that the crucifixion is a historical fact. And how can someone who is so special as to be born of a virgin and who would even come back to the world be just a prophet of God and no more? I have raised objections against the very sensual image of heaven in the Koran (which says that people in heaven will get beautiful virgins and stuff like that) and have compared that against the biblical view that heaven is just a re-union with God and that hell is basically a separation from God. We have argued about a lot of other things too.

But the most painful discovery for me about the Islamic faith has been the concept of militancy. I always used to think that these fanatics were just misguided people who give Islam a bad name. To be sure, Islam does not permit killing of innocent women and children but as I have found out, its teachings are quite different from those of Jesus who wants you to turn the other cheek. Islam says it's much better to forgive, but you do have the right to take revenge. Jesus absolutely insists on forgiveness.

My understanding is that according to the Christian faith and that saying of Jesus, the forgiveness of our sins is conditional upon us forgiving other people. In this regard, your book, *The Jesus I Never Knew* was quite illuminating, along with the very theological *On Being a Christian* by Hans Küng. As I know now, violence does have a strong precedent in Islam and the Koran does encourage warfare in some circumstances. Not all those circumstances call for defensive war either. As I have read the Koran recently and its explanations, and the life history of prophet Muhammad, I have found out that the concept of political domination by force is very prevalent in it. And the terrible tragedy that happened yesterday in this country—to me it seems the logical outcome of the teachings which tell you it's OK to reply in kind, that you are duty bound to enforce the will of God through warfare if necessary. I could be wrong here in my opinion, but I think that's what happens when you try to enforce God's will in this earthly world rather than believing that your kingdom is not of this world but of the other world.

I realize that I have put my parents in an extremely painful situation. My mom is so distressed. She has been pleading with me not to abandon my faith. I love her so very much. I can't put in words how much I love her. And she loves me even more than that. But I just don't know what to do. How can I force my heart to believe in something which just doesn't seem right to me? It seems I am in a no-win situation. I still have a lot of questions about Christian beliefs, but I know that if I decide to convert I will be causing an immense amount of heartbreak. And that is the last thing I want to do. It would be like giving up everything I grew up with. I would be ostracized by all my relatives, they would be just so shocked and scandalized. Also, my legal status in this country expires next year. Considering my views about Islam now and my sympathetic and favorable view about the Christian faith, I can't imagine going back to Pakistan. It would be just impossible. But how would I manage to stay here in this country? Do you think there is a way?

Do you think I would find loving and open-minded friends in the church? Would it be fair to say some people would put their guards up and won't want anything to do with someone who belongs to some different Asian-Indian race? Someone who has a different color of skin and speaks with an accent?

My mom came here to visit with strong hopes of arranging my marriage here to someone from our culture. But what girl from our culture can even think of marrying someone who is not a Muslim anymore? I have dashed my mom's hope, I feel I am letting her down. Above all, she is so extremely distressed by the fact that, according to Islamic teachings and the Koran, anyone who leaves Islam and converts to another faith is going to burn in hell forever. She says she can't even begin to imagine that. And I can understand her pain.

I am in pain and immense confusion myself. My family thinks I have gone a little crazy. I don't know, maybe they are right. I know for sure that if I decide to convert I am going to suffer a lot of consequences. I can't really predict what is going to happen since someone converting to another faith is totally without any precedent in our family and all the people we know. But then I think of that Jesus saying, What is the use if you gain this life and lose the life which really matters. But you see, it's not just about my life. Do I have the right to hurt my parents so much who raised me with so much sacrifice and devotion? I really am so confused, so lost. Please tell me what to do. God bless you.

*I have been corresponding with the author of this letter ever since. He is still torn between what he believes in his head and what he feels in his heart—the rupture that it would cause his family if he converted to Christianity.*

Chapter 15

# Why Do They Hate Us?

After September 11 and two subsequent wars, Americans have been asking that question about Muslims. President Bush voiced it with a tone of bewilderment. We Americans think of ourselves as generous, optimistic, and fair, so it comes as a shock to realize that we inspire hatred strong enough to incite mass murder.

The results of a survey conducted by the Princeton Survey Research Associates underscore the gulf between Americans' perceptions and the rest of the world's. Whereas only 18 percent of Americans considered "U.S. policies and actions in the world" a main cause of terrorist attacks against us, elsewhere that figure rose to 58 percent, and to 81 percent in the Middle East.

I recently listened to a panel of international experts and American luminaries address the question, "Why do they hate us?" in an all-day forum. A British management consultant and an

American Pulitzer Prize–winning historian answered with an attitude approaching resignation. "What's new? Others always resent the top dog. Look at the history of empires, the haves vs. the have-nots."

To my surprise, the lone Pakistani on the panel defended the U.S. "Only Americans would even convene a panel like this," he said. "Look at what the French and British empires did. When their subjects criticized them, they imprisoned or shot them. Wherever I go, Americans are trying to learn more about Islam and are critically examining their own country. It amazes me." He also observed that terrorists had to launch their attack on American soil because the U.S. does not occupy other countries, a policy that terrorism, ironically, changed.

An American university professor made an analogy to which many nodded assent. She cited one of her colleagues who had stopped dating undergraduate coeds because, he said, "It's like giving aid to a Third World country. You do everything for them, and then they end up hating you."

On the other hand, participants noted examples that made some sense of Muslim hatred. Diplomats brought up American policy in the Middle East; we are, after all, the source for the helicopter gunships and jet fighters used by Israelis against the Palestinians.

One panelist mentioned the *Baywatch* syndrome. That long-running television program, which featured hunks and babes cavorting on the beaches of California, replaced *Dallas* as the most popular U.S. television export overseas. "We are attracted to what we most fear," said a thoughtful Muslim panelist. "Imagine what decadent American culture represents to a young Muslim who, outside his family, has never seen a woman's knee, or even her face."

The French sociologist Jacques Ellul noted a paradoxical trend that the Christian gospel tends to produce values in society that directly contradict that gospel. Internationally, the United States is known for its great wealth, military power, and sexual license—all three of which run directly counter to Jesus' teaching.

When Samuel Huntington first raised the specter of a "clash of civilizations," many experts greeted his prophecy with derision. Not so long ago, most Islamic nations were championing the ideal of a secular state. Now, fundamentalists are on the ascendancy, vigorously resisting some cardinal values of the West: human rights, democracy, sexual equality, capitalism, a scientific worldview, religious pluralism.

Most Americans understand the difference between a committed Christian who accepts Jesus as a model for living and a "cultural Christian" who happens to live in a nation that has a Christian heritage. Not everyone overseas can make that distinction. Much of the world draws conclusions about "the Christian West" by watching MTV, *Baywatch*, and violent movies. Muslims speak of nuclear weapons as "the Christian bomb." (When asked if he would let his children become Christians, Mahatma Gandhi replied, "Yes, if they don't drink Scotch whiskey and eat beef"—even he identified Christianity with a European culture that permitted what was forbidden to Hindus.)

Perhaps American Christians should give more attention to the "clash of civilizations" closer to home, the inevitable conflict between two overlapping kingdoms. Living in a decadent Roman empire sixteen hundred years ago, Augustine of Hippo made a crucial distinction between "the city of God" and what he called "the city of man." We hold a dual citizenship, he said, and must carefully weigh whether loyalty to one conflicts with loyalty to the other.

Some in the United States judge our nation's success by such measures as gross national product, military might, and global dominance. The kingdom of God measures such things as care for the downtrodden and love for enemies. We must not forget that Jesus' parable of the sheep and the goats in Matthew 25 presents a judgment of the *nations*. In that final reckoning, God judges nations by how they treat the poor, the sick, the hungry, the alien, and the prisoner.

Even as the U.S. government pursues the war against terrorism, perhaps we Christians should launch our own private war—not against terrorists, but against their breeding ground. We can increase giving to organizations like Prison Fellowship International and the International Justice Mission, which act out globally the lessons of Matthew 25; and to World Vision and the Salvation Army, which show "Western values" in a different light; and to International Students, which works to link international students with American Christian hosts. How differently would the world view us if it associated the U.S. with the "Jesus syndrome" rather than the "*Baywatch* syndrome"?

Chapter 16

# The Great Divide

In recent times Americans have watched on television as mobs of screaming Muslims, calling for "death to the Great Satan," burn our presidents in effigy. The geography of protest changes—first Iran and Libya, then Lebanon, then on to such places as Iraq and Afghanistan—but the zealousness does not. Some religious fanatics out there genuinely despise us.

Most Americans do not know what to make of these scenes. Our political leaders seem to us more like congenial uncles than tyrants. The label "Great Satan" especially rankles, for we think of the U.S. as a Christian nation, far more devout than, say, Western Europe. At least we still go to church. How can anyone imagine us as pagan?

A great divide has opened up again between the world's two largest religions, Christianity and Islam. In the previous century we grew so accustomed to the polarity of communism versus capitalism, we forgot that the Western world was once obsessed with a polarity of religion. It behooves us to understand each other lest we stumble into another eight-hundred-year conflict.

Islamic criticisms of the West often center on the fusty word *materialism*. When that word describes the pursuit of wealth and consumer comforts, few Arab nations disapprove: thanks to oil revenues, the Persian Gulf is one of the wealthiest regions in the world. But materialism also refers to a philosophical approach, a belief that human life consists mainly (or solely) in what takes place here and now, in the world of matter.

The disciples of Islam tend to view the West as being obsessively concerned with this life, not the eternity to come. One reason Saddam Hussein gambled on an invasion of Kuwait was that he doubted the West, and the U.S. in particular, had the will to risk thousands of lives in a war. In contrast, the conflict between Iran and Iraq had already proved that hundreds of thousands of faithful Muslims would gladly die in "glorious martyrdom" if promised instant passage into paradise. Subsequently, Europe and the United States have learned along with Israel that there is really no foolproof defense against suicide bombers.

In an irony of history, Islam has now co-opted the word *martyr*. Early Christians prevailed over Rome because they opted for eternal rewards instead of mere physical survival. They refused to renounce their faith, and the blood of the martyrs became the seeds of the church. (A key difference: the Christians were dying at the hands of Rome, not killing anyone else.) Nowadays you hear very little talk in the West about eternal rewards and much talk about techniques to keep death at bay. Young Arabs who study here come away impressed with, and often scandalized by, how much energy we invest in the physical life. Scout the magazine racks at a local drugstore sometime, counting the titles devoted to bodybuilding, diet, fashion, and naked women—all emblems of the prominence we give to materiality.

*Puritanical* is another Christian word co-opted by Islamic societies. While fighting in the two Gulf Wars, for the first time in recent memory U.S. soldiers had to get by without alcohol and *Playboy*, in deference to the strict Islamic code in the staging nations. Few of them realized, however, that the difference in moral standards between Islam and the West is philosophical, not just cultural.

In determining morality, American society tends to apply the bottom-line principle, "Does it hurt anyone else?" Thus pornography is legal, but not if it involves explicit violence or child molestation. You can get legally drunk as long as you do not break a neighbor's window or drive a car, endangering others. Violence on television is okay, because everyone knows the characters are just acting.

This yardstick of morality betrays our implicit materialism. Whereas we define "hurt" in the most physical terms, Islamic societies see it in more spiritual terms. In that deeper sense, what could be more harmful than divorce, say, or pornography, or violence-as-entertainment, or even the cynical depiction of banal evil on television soap operas? It is from this vantage point that the U.S. has gained its reputation as "the Great Satan."

The same materialism shows through in our preferred methods of punishment. Americans are scandalized by such Islamic "brutalities" as beheadings, public beatings, and the amputation of thieves' hands. How could they be so cruel? we wonder. But we lock teenagers in cells crowded with abusive criminals; do we ever ponder what happens to their souls? "Do not be afraid of those who kill the body but cannot kill the soul," Jesus cautioned. And again, "It is better for you to lose one part of your body than for your whole body to go to hell."

The Italian writer Umberto Eco (*The Name of the Rose, Foucault's Pendulum*) wrote a fascinating account of a trip across America titled *Travels in Hyperreality*. He too came away impressed with our basic materialism. Americans even give physical substance to their myths, he observed. Ancient Greeks celebrated their heroes in song and poetry around a campfire; Americans shake hands with them in fuzzy suits at Disneyland.

Religious television intrigued Eco: "If you follow the Sunday morning religious programs on TV you come to understand that God can be experienced only as nature, flesh, energy, tangible image. And since no preacher dares show us God in the form of a bearded dummy, or as a Disneyland robot, God can only be found in the form of natural force, joy, healing, youth, health, economic increment." Where is the *mysterium tremendum*, Eco wondered; where is the holy, numinous, ineffable God?

I must confess that of the major world religions, Islam is hardest for me to understand and appreciate. I find its doctrine unconvincing and its fanaticism terrifying. Yet questions raised by Islam should trouble us Christians in the West. Islam has, above all, cherished the belief in a holy, numinous God. It has also nourished a profound allegiance to a spiritual and immortal life, not just a material and mortal one. We "infidels" have some lessons to learn.

# Chapter 17

# Does It Matter
# What Others Think?

During the war with Iraq, I heard a caller on a Christian radio station suggest, "Why don't we just raze the United
Nations Headquarters in New York and rebuild the
World Trade Center on that site!" The host enthusiastically
agreed. For the next hour, callers piled on scorn for France, Germany, and other nations that had "wimpy" objections to the war,
and they dismissed all Arab concerns out of hand. The U.S., they
seemed to imply, has the right, even the obligation, to go it alone
in bringing order to the world.

Because I frequently travel overseas, I am struck by the difference in how Americans perceive themselves and how those of
other nations see us. Some who live overseas see us as arrogant,
selfish, decadent, and uncaring. They judge American values by
our rap music and television shows, most of which glorify sex,
wealth, and violence. They know that the U.S. military possesses

more weapons of mass destruction than all other armies combined. And they note that the world's wealthiest nation contributes only half as much foreign aid as Europe.

The outpouring of sympathy after September 11 demonstrated that the U.S., for all its faults, could still draw on a large reservoir of goodwill. WE ARE ALL AMERICANS NOW, proclaimed one headline. The fact that the newspaper was the largest in *France* shows how much of that goodwill has since dissipated.

I heard the former ambassador to the U.S. from Pakistan, a devoted friend of America, put it this way: "In the days of the Cold War, there were two giants on the world stage—a brutal giant and a gentle giant. Now there is only one giant, and we fear it becoming brutal."

Even our closest allies view the U.S. as a loner nation which pulls out of treaties that don't serve our interests. We backed out of the Kyoto Accords, the Law of the Sea, and the International Criminal Court, as well as treaties controlling land mines and chemical weapons. The callers on the talk shows recounted some of those reversals with pride. "Who needs the rest of the world?" asked one.

Well, we need the rest of the world, as the war in Iraq made clear. When television broadcast the Iraqis' abuse of our POWs, we appealed to the Geneva Convention. When rumors spread about illicit weapons, we threatened an international war crimes tribunal. As bills for reconstruction mounted, we turned to other nations for help in relieving Iraq's debt.

I hope and pray that our military presence in the Middle East leads to stability in the region and reduced terrorism globally. I fear just the opposite, that sowing the wind may reap the whirlwind.

A friend of mine traveling in Malaysia brought back a newspaper report of a speech by the prime minister there. Right now, we cannot stop the U.S. from doing whatever it wants, admitted

Malaysia's leader. Their power is that great. Our only hope is to produce our own weapons, our own "Islamic bomb." Then we can stand up to the giant.

My concerns come in part from discussions with the one group of conservative Christians most nervous about anti-Americanism: missionaries. They bear the brunt of world opinion, and sometimes pay for it with their lives. One wrote, "Arabs are interpreting war against Iraq as Christian aggression against an Islamic nation. This false perception is so deeply ingrained among most Arabs that it undermines any perception of Christianity as a message of love and peace."

As the world's only superpower, the United States bears grave responsibilities of leadership. Sometimes we must use force, and sometimes restraint. Sometimes we must act against world opinion. Popular psychiatrist M. Scott Peck makes an intriguing observation, however:

> It is notable that two hundred years ago this new nation
> spent virtually no money and no energy attempting to
> control the behavior of the other nations of the world. Yet
> one by one, almost ten by ten, the peoples of these nations
> followed our spiritual and political example to seek the same
> freedoms for themselves. It is hard to escape the conclusion
> that in the years since, our political and spiritual leadership
> has declined in inverse proportion to the increasing amounts
> of money and effort we have expended to manipulate other
> countries. . . . I wonder, if we in the United States were to
> concentrate—as our overwhelmingly major priority—on
> making ourselves the best possible society we can be,
> whether the nations of the world might once again, without
> any pressure except the influence of example, begin to
> emulate us.

# Chapter 18

# Abraham, Jesus, and Muhammad in New Orleans

Occasionally I get invited to unusual gatherings as a result of my writing. One of the most memorable took place in New Orleans at the invitation of M. Scott Peck, psychiatrist and author of such books as *The Road Less Traveled* and *People of the Lie*. Peck has a theory that the process of building community must precede the resolution of disagreements, and he brought together thirty disparate people in order to test that theory.

Peck convened ten Christians, ten Jews, and ten Muslims, a microcosm representing perhaps the most fractious disagreement of Western civilization. The central issue that shadowed us was, "Can people with fundamentally different truth claims live together without killing each other?" We met at a Catholic retreat center the weekend before Mardi Gras. (Try explaining the Christian roots of that booze-and-sex bash to followers of another religion.) For three days we discussed, well, whatever we wanted to discuss.

Certain cultural differences surfaced right away. Scott Peck conducts his community-building workshops according to a formula that calls for introspective "I" statements and personal sharing, and the Jews responded warmly to this approach. "Don't forget, we invented psychotherapy," joked one rabbi. Muslim participants, though, showed little enthusiasm. One imam tried to explain: "We have a cultural aversion to psychotherapy. You'll rarely hear a Muslim talk about personal problems. It just isn't done."

As a result, we Christians frequently found ourselves on the sidelines watching Muslims respond to the Jews' self-questioning musings with fixed pronouncements of absolute truth. These in turn provoked even more "I" statements from the Jews and more pronouncements from the Muslims. It felt good to be on the sidelines, actually; Christians don't have a very good history with either of these religions, and I much preferred our new mediator role to past pogroms and crusades.

I learned a new word in New Orleans, *supersessionism,* which helped me understand the Muslims' apparent aplomb. The Jews resented the notion that Christian faith had *superseded* Judaism. "I feel like a curiosity of history, as if my religion should be put in a nursing home," said one. "It grates on me to hear the term 'Old Testament God' or even the word 'Old' Testament, for that matter." I had to agree that Christianity has a frankly supersessionist aspect. Jesus introduced the "new covenant" even as he transformed the Jewish Passover seder into what Christians now call "the Lord's Supper." Later, the apostle Paul referred to the Old Testament law as a "tutor" or "schoolmaster" to lead us to Christ.

I had not realized, however, that Muslims look on both faiths with a supersessionist attitude. As they see it, just as Christianity grew out of and incorporated parts of Judaism, Islam grew out of and incorporated parts of both religions. Abraham was a prophet;

Jesus was a prophet; but Muhammad was The Prophet. The Old Testament has a place, as does the New Testament, but the Koran is "the final revelation." Hearing my own faith talked about with such condescension gave me insight into how Jews have felt for two millennia.

Ironically, it was the common language of pain that seemed to bring the three groups together. Many of the Jewish participants had lost family members in the Holocaust, and some had also served as volunteers in Israel's wars against Arab neighbors. On the Muslim side, one woman told of the horrors that descended upon her once-lovely neighborhood in Beirut, Lebanon. Another Muslim gave a wrenching account of the Deir Yassin massacre in 1948, when members of the Israeli Stern gang killed 250 members of his village and threw their bodies in a well. He, at the age of ten, was fleet enough to escape. But a soldier shot his two-year-old brother and ninety-six-year-old grandmother in cold blood.

Suffering sometimes serves as a moat and sometimes as a bridge. The Muslim who fled from the soldiers at Deir Yassin years later had an automobile accident in the United States. It was a Jewish nurse who stopped, tied a tourniquet with her scented hanky, and painstakingly plucked glass from his face. He believes she saved his life. The Muslim man's wife, a physician, went on to say that she had once treated a patient with a strange tattoo on his wrist. When she asked about it, he told her about the Holocaust, a historical event omitted from her high school, college, and graduate school education in Arab countries. For the first time, she understood Jewish pain.

Why do human beings keep doing it to each other? Yugoslavia, Ireland, Sudan, the West Bank—is there no end to the cycle of pain fueled by religion? As Gandhi observed, the logic of "an eye for an eye, a tooth for a tooth" cannot sustain itself forever; ultimately both parties end up blind and toothless.

Our meeting in New Orleans did not, rest assured, change the Middle East equation or make peace between three major religions any more likely. But it did change us. For once we focused on intersections and connections, not just boundaries. We got to know Hillel, Dawud, and Bob, human faces behind the labels Jew, Muslim, and Christian.

Each faith held a worship service—Muslims on Friday, Jews on Saturday, Christians on Sunday—to which the others were invited as observers. The Muslim worship service consisted mostly of reverential prayers to the Almighty. The Jewish service consisted of readings from Psalms and the Torah and some warm-hearted singing. We Christians celebrated the Lord's Supper and told of how it helps us to look back to Christ's death, to look forward to his return, and to live in the present, a state of grace made possible by his body, broken for us.

All three services had striking similarities and reminded us how much the three faiths have in common. Perhaps the intensity of feeling among the three traditions stems from a common heritage: family disputes are always the stubbornest, and civil wars the bloodiest.

One rabbi gave this response to the weekend. "I did not want to come here. I almost canceled. Ten days ago I was visiting Auschwitz. I stood where so many thousands died—just for the crime of being Jewish. At Auschwitz, some Catholics asked me to pray with them. How could I? I knew that the Catholic Church had remained silent while members of my family were forced to dig their own graves.

"I wasn't ready to meet with Christians and Muslims so soon. I could not get past my own pain. This weekend has been hard for me, and yet now I can say I am glad I came. It was the pain of healing I have felt, not the pain of fresh wounds.

"A few of us have now heard each other's stories. We have been affected. Yet the institutions we represent keep on hating, keep on murdering. Can what happens this weekend produce anything more than a beautiful experience for the few of us who have gathered? Is there any way for the systems themselves to change, any way to break the cycle?"

The rabbi had circled back to the summary question of the weekend: "Can people with fundamentally different truth claims live together without killing each other?" That, sadly, is a question that cannot be answered by one weekend in New Orleans.

# Chapter 19

# Along the Frontier

The sky turned first an eerie yellow, then the color of charcoal. A gritty rain began to fall, coating windshields, sidewalks, and clothing with damp spots the color and consistency of white clay. It was Libya we were feeling, its sands swept up in a freak storm, the worst in a quarter century, and blown across the Mediterranean to be deposited on Cyprus. I was there attending a conference of Christians involved in media, and the sandstorm seemed a poignant symbol of the siege mentality of Christians in the region.

To the south and east Cyprus faces hundreds of millions of Muslims; from the north, Turkey has invaded and still occupies a third of the island. Flags emblazoned with the Muslim crescent flap defiantly over church buildings seized from the hilltops around Nicosia. Only a thin line of UN peacekeepers keeps the two sides from breaking into war again.

Christian workers at the conference had gathered to discuss

new ways of reaching the Muslim world. They used pseudonyms to throw off Muslim agents who might be tailing them. In restaurants and public places they spoke in hushed tones and glanced around frequently. They left no notes lying about after their closed meetings.

Like inverted mushrooms, satellite dishes have sprouted on Arab rooftops, and Christian programs are now beaming into places like Saudi Arabia, Iraq, and the slums of Cairo. Syria recently resigned itself to the inevitable, and Internet providers are now bringing Christian websites into private homes there. Christian ministries receive letters like these: "Should I tell my parents that I have become a Christian? It is a capital crime here to convert, and they could have me executed. What do you advise?"

The region's largest nation, Egypt, has long tolerated a strong Christian minority. As I visited, evangelicals were celebrating the success of a nontraditional Luis Palau crusade. Unable to rent stadiums for an evangelistic event, they organized hundreds of churches to run proxy crusades by videotape. Palau himself appeared at a large Presbyterian church in Cairo; after a hectic night's work by volunteers, videotapes of that service were shown the next day in churches, halls, and open courtyards at five hundred sites across Egypt.

Ironically, young Christians see some advantages to living in a Muslim culture. As one told me, "We have restrictions, yes, but we and the Moslems have lived together for centuries. I have gone to the U.S. to study, but certainly I would not want to raise a family there. Here we have no pornography, little premarital sex or alcohol, and I feel safe walking on the streets. As long as I have the freedom to worship, I prefer living in Egypt."

The same young person, though, admitted that he seldom attends the Coptic church in which he was baptized. The service, after all, is conducted in Old Coptic, a language no one in the congregation understands. It lasts several hours, during most of which the congregation stands, and is filled with obscure iconic symbolism. There is no such thing as a "seeker-driven" church in the Middle East. Most countries outlaw proselytism, and without fresh blood the churches tend to rely on familiar rituals, shunning innovation.

Lebanon, like Egypt, was once known for its amicable blending of different faiths. That was before religious groups formed private militias and began killing each other. Over 150,000 died in a civil war that lasted fifteen years, and many buildings in Beirut still bear the scars of shrapnel and bullet holes.

Psychological scars go much deeper. A visiting American told me he attended a basketball game that referees had to interrupt because of fighting—among the opposing fans, not the players. "They cleared the entire arena, except for a handful of us foreigners. The players resumed the game and the fans went into the street to continue their brawl."

A twenty-year-old in Lebanon cannot shed the memories of war. For years, every time she drove to a church event, she had to pass through two or three army checkpoints. How does she forget the memories: a decapitated head mounted on the hood of a Mercedes; a sniper being dragged through the streets, his feet tied to a bumper, his head bouncing grotesquely on the pavement.

"Christian" militias were as notorious for their cruelty as their Muslim counterparts. Today in Beirut the most prevalent Christian shrines are devoted to Elijah. You see the prophet in churches, at intersections, on street corners, always portrayed with a sword in his hand. Pilgrims bring him flowers and kiss the statue. Elijah, after all, slew 850 false prophets (at a site just down the highway). They acknowledge Jesus as the central figure of faith, but Elijah makes a far more impressive militia mascot.

In Lebanon, I met a woman who had pored over my book

*Disappointment with God* by candlelight in the basement as bombs were destroying her building. And another who is actively trying to apply principles from *What's So Amazing about Grace?* to her neighbors: "squatters" who commandeered her apartment and who regularly siphon off her water and electricity supplies. As I remember my trip to the Middle East, I think how easy it is to write about the gospel from my serene perch in Colorado, and how hard to put it into practice on its home turf—now the literal frontier of faith.

Part Four

✠

Finding

God

in

a

Fractured

Society

# Chapter 20

# Eccentric on the Front Lines

His breath reeking of alcohol, a grizzled, rheumy-eyed old man wearing a torn high school letter jacket sticks out his hand and slurs through a monologue about needing bus money. His story sounds cockamamie, and your street wisdom tells you where a donation would likely go. Maybe you should offer to take him to a restaurant, or to a rescue mission. But you don't. You shake your head, thrust your hands into your pockets, and keep walking.

You bump into people like him whenever you go downtown. Inside, it nags at you. Mother Teresa or John Wesley or Dwight L. Moody would not walk away. They'd do something about the man, even if it meant founding a ministry to take care of needs like his. "The face of Jesus in most distressing disguise," Mother Teresa once called the beggars of Calcutta. She got that right. Most distressing indeed.

By the end of the day, rationalization has papered over any lingering guilt. After all, you had important business to tend to. You can't possibly *respond to all human needs. And other people specialize in ministries to street people—maybe you'll contribute some money to them.*

*Even so, you wonder. What would it look like if a Christian took literally Jesus' sweeping commands and acted on them. What would a Good Samaritan look like today, in urban America?*

Such a person might look like Louise Adamson, a friend in Atlanta has told you. She's a missionary, but unlike any missionary you may have met before. She is more like a full-time Good Samaritan. You must meet her, he says. And so you do meet her, in a cramped office of an aging Presbyterian church in the shadow of a baseball stadium slated for demolition.

The furniture is government-issue hand-me-down. The carpet smells like the scrapings off the soles of thirty years' worth of shoes. Louise is in her sixties, you reckon. She has an ample nose, strong, straight teeth, a pitted complexion, a full head of graying hair. She is wearing a simple purple dress that could have come out of any decade but this one. Her voice cracks as she talks, giving the impression that she's on the verge of tears. (Possibly a true impression: you start keeping track of the times she does burst into tears, and the count soon reaches thirteen.)

You have much leisure time to make these observations, for Louise talks nonstop. Forty-five minutes ago you asked a simple question, and she is still going strong. Listening to Louise is like moving the dial from one radio station to another, eavesdropping on talk shows that are all covering unrelated topics. The difference is that Louise, not you, controls the dial.

"Louise, tell me about yourself," was how you began forty-five minutes ago, and she started at birth, recounting her life in the rather odd lilt of an Old Testament prophet. "I am like Gideon, the least of the house of Manasseh, called out of a cornfield, a cotton patch . . ." The cotton patch lay in North Georgia, which is where Louise grew up. She changes topics a few times, but eventually circles back to her health complications in childhood.

"I had double pneumonia three times before I reached the age of six, and very often a black couple would come to relieve my parents' nursing duties. Our house had no racial prejudice, none whatever. One night my lung collapsed, and my eyes rolled back in my head, and no one thought I would make it through the night. A neighbor offered to dig my grave. But—I believe it was a miracle—I woke up in the middle of the night, started breathing, and announced I wanted corn bread and cabbage. I still remember what Mother said. She said, 'Louise, you're not your own. God saved you for a purpose. Seek it out.' "

The tears start flowing. The memory has triggered a deep emotional response in Louise. "Oh, the Lord's ways are so beautiful, incomprehensible, so past finding out."

You use the segue to interject a second question: "Is that when you felt called to serve God?" Immediately you learn about Louise's unconventional approach to interpreting the Bible. "You know how Isaiah 40 says 'Wait upon the Lord'? Well, I've taken that as my motto. I want to wait on the Lord like a waitress waiting on tables. I want to serve him every day." And suddenly she has leaped forward twenty years and is describing her student days in Atlanta.

In the 1940s, while working full-time and going to evening school three nights a week, Louise volunteered for mission work in the slums of Atlanta, African-American neighborhoods with colorful names like Buttermilk Basin and Cabbagetown. "I would hold Bible clubs for the children. Most of the houses were built on stilts or concrete blocks, and when it rained we would sweep aside the cobwebs and climb up underneath the houses to hold our meetings. It was there that God opened up to me the great face of missions—the heartache, the sadness, the need. But I knew I needed more training, so after I finished my college courses I enrolled in a Southern Baptist seminary."

You have been warned that Louise is something of a pack rat, and sure enough she reaches under a table and hauls out a huge cardboard box of yellowed newspapers. She has marked feature articles that graphically describe those postwar slums, and she reads these aloud. Once again the tears flow. "Listen to this. Three girls, ages 7, 9, and 11. Their mother, a prostitute, ties them to her bed for men to molest. Can you imagine it? It was just a massive sea of suffering in those days. The rest of the world went on as if the people in those neighborhoods did not exist. They were like the thirteenth tribe of Israel, a lost tribe. This was the greatest slum south of Chicago."

Louise has a detailed inner map of the changing sociology of the city, but it bears little resemblance to what you might read in a sociology textbook. It goes like this. "In the 1950s, the inner city began to envelop the main churches. God was standing there saying to us, 'Don't run! Stay! I have brought the masses to you.' Like I once heard from a black preacher, God said to Moses at the edge of the Red Sea, 'Don't just do something—stand there!' And that's what God was telling the church, just to stand.

"But we didn't stand, most of us. We ran. And so in the 1960s rioters started burning those cities down. God wanted his people to lower the racial barriers, to overcome the differences, to open the doors. If we wouldn't do it on our own, others would do it for us.

"And then in the 1970s, God said, 'The church hasn't met the challenge of the fifties and the sixties, so I'll move on with my Spirit in my own way.' That's when the Jesus movement broke out, and there came a new outpouring of God's Spirit. God was so far ahead of us that many people never have caught up."

During those decades, Louise tried not to get left in the dust. She had found a husband in the seminary, and he took the pastorate at a large inner-city church, all white, in what Atlantans like to call a "changing neighborhood." The neighborhood was changing far too fast for most white tastes, and the church was divided over whether to integrate racially. The issue of black membership finally came to a head at a fractious congregational meeting.

Louise remembers it well. "I was so proud of my husband and the stand he took. The church was packed. Conservatives had recruited scores of members still on the rolls who hadn't been to church in years. We voted by secret ballot, and by a margin of 39 votes they decided to keep black people out. My husband resigned, and we lost everything—our income, the parsonage, everything. And you know something, I think the Spirit of God left the church that day. It started dying from that day on. Those were dark times, when we wondered if God had abandoned the city."

Four years later Louise's husband died. She stayed in the neighborhood, living on a modest income provided through the Southern Baptist Home Mission Board. In the 1970s she mostly worked with children, teaching fifteen hundred a week in Bible classes. As she got to know the children, she got to know their needs. Soon she was distributing food and clothing, appearing at the juvenile court as a character witness, visiting hospitals and prisons. If Louise came across children from abusive families, she would ask their parents to let the children move in with her. In this way she has been "mother" to some fourteen children. "Isn't God good! He knew exactly what he was doing by not giving me any children of my own. I would have been so burdened down I wouldn't be there for these precious little ones.

"I never planned a formal 'ministry.' My goodness! God would just bring these wonderful people into my life. The Baptist Church allowed me to use their facilities on weekdays, as long as no blacks came on Sunday. One day I brought in a little black girl who had just accepted Jesus. She asked the pastor if she could be baptized, and the church went into a kind of panic. Within two months the congregation had moved to Stone Mountain, twenty miles east of Atlanta.

"But for some reason the Baptists kept sending me support, and soon a Presbyterian church opened its doors. They gave me their keys and said, 'Louise, you can bring anybody you want into our church—black, yellow, prostitute, alcoholic, anybody.' Isn't it marvelous how God provides? Remember that psalm about the pit and the miry clay? God's still rescuing people out of the pit, and it's too bad some of these churches didn't stick around and get to know them."

All this time, Louise had to file official reports with the Southern Baptist Home Mission Board. Her method of ministry did not fit any of their established categories. Louise calls her ministry a "Jericho Road ministry," after the parable of the Good Samaritan, who helped a man left for dead on the road to Jericho. "I don't have a board or committee, or anything like that. I used to work through local churches, but they all kept moving away. I just work on my own. People give me food and clothing, and I distribute it around."

Louise gets a little testy when questioned about planning and organization. "How would anyone go about scheduling a Jericho Road ministry? You just walk down the road and look for victims, and it may be daylight before you ever reach Jericho. You can't structure people's crises. They hit with no warning, like a tornado. And I've been here so long, lots of these people call me before they call the police or fire department. We've made missions so difficult, don't you think? It's just a matter of living for God, and loving those around you. The Lord structures my every day. And at the end of every day I feel like falling on my knees to sing the Hallelujah Chorus."

The Presbyterian church finally closed down too, after its congregation had shrunk to a few dozen members. They asked Louise to keep using the building, hoping that her presence might discourage vandalism. She practically moved into the run-down sanctuary, holding her Bible classes there, teaching unwed mothers, giving shelter to the homeless. Eventually, a few young professional Christians with a social conscience moved into the neighborhood, and the church revived. "You see," Louise says triumphantly, "God never left this place! He was here all along."

You listen to stories from Louise all afternoon. As the sun starts to drop below the trees outside, you feel moved and inspired, but still you have only the vaguest picture of how Louise actually spends her time. What happened yesterday, for example, or today? Does she just wake up in the morning and wait for the phone to ring? You interrupt her and ask that question.

"Morning? No, no, it usually rings at night. Let's see—yesterday. Oh, yes. A mother I'd been working with called me around supper time. I went right over and found her sitting in the middle of the floor with bruises all over her face. Her husband had been beating her again. She had a big bottle of prescription medicine beside her on the floor, and she told me she'd been fighting all day not to take it. Two kids were crying their lungs out in the next room. I had brought some groceries with me, so we cooked a dinner, calmed the kids down, and spent two hours cleaning house together. By the end of that time we were both singing hymns as we worked.

"When I got home, the fatigue set in. I got another call about midnight. Three elderly people had been shut up in a house for three days without food. My first response was, 'Lord, I'm tired. I want to go to bed.' But Jesus said to love your neighbor as yourself, and if that was my mother in that apartment, I'd want someone to feed her. So I went to the store right quick. They lived on the third floor. Dragging those groceries up the first two flights, I felt bone-tired. But somewhere about the second-floor landing, it was like God hit me with a shot of B-12. I went in and spent three hours with those lovely ladies. We had a banquet in the middle of the night. I was so excited I could hardly fall asleep when I went home."

What about burnout? "Well, sure, I get tired, and when it gets too bad I head up to the farm in North Georgia for a week or so. But Jesus said to seek first the kingdom of God, and all these things will be added unto you. And you know something, that's true. Sometimes discouraging things happen. Last year my house was broken into three times. I usually know who did it—kids after money for drugs. Last time it was two kids I've tried to help for years. I tracked them down, told them that of course I wouldn't press charges, and asked if I could pray with them. The best thing happened. I heard from the one boy's mother that her son told her, 'Miz Adamson, she bugs us. I break into her house, and she comes back with a load of food and a Bible. That bugs me.' Now isn't that great! If he'd gone to prison he would come out so mad you could never reach him for Jesus. Now he can't get Jesus out of his mind!"

Louise is crying again, and when she stops, she tells another story, about one of her foster children. She currently serves as official guardian for twelve children assigned to her by the juvenile court. You listen to these stories until the sun disappears completely and the lights come on and it is time to go. On the street outside, after you have said good-bye to Louise and after she has prayed aloud for your safe journey home, you run into one of the fourteen children that Louise has raised.

The girl's name is Faye, and when you tell her you've spent the afternoon with Louise, she begins talking excitedly, just like Louise. "What a woman. Every day I pray, 'Lord, teach me to be more like Louise. Teach me to love people and not be so selfish.' I was eight years old when I moved in with Louise, and I had no idea what love was. We lived in a tenement with the lights and gas cut off and my dad in prison. When my little brother was burned all over in a fire we'd lit to keep warm, Louise offered to help out by raising me. For the first time in my life I was with someone who wasn't afraid to touch me and hug me. She told me that the most important thing in life was that Jesus loved me, and then she put arms to his love. She'd wake me up at three in the morning, say, 'Come on, honey, we've got to go.' I would sleep in a pallet on the floorboard of the car while she ran in to check on somebody who had just got burned out of her home.

"I had a sister who stomped out of home thirteen years ago and said, 'I'm never coming back to this God-forsaken place.' She was chasing wealth, and married a boy she thought would make her rich. It didn't work out. Her kids are right back here, strung out on dope. But I guess the thing I learned most from Louise was that God has not forsaken this place. Not by a long shot. He's still here."

Louise Adamson is a true eccentric. Her house blends in well in the neighborhood she serves. Old sofas clutter the front porch (waiting for placement with needy refugees). Rattletrap cars sit on the front lawn (soon to be donated to poor families). She doesn't fit the pattern of any minister or social worker you know. She has no staff or organized program. She doesn't give tax deductible receipts to her donors (although for years she has faithfully saved all her own receipts—in a large pasteboard box in her living room). If you asked her about a five-year plan, or even a five-day plan, she would stare at you blankly. She says she needs to stay free to listen to God's Spirit. She simply wakes up each day and asks God to use her.

Meanwhile, in university offices sociologists analyze the cycle of dependency in the underclass. In seminaries, urban specialists devise strategies to address the problems of the inner city. Government task forces study the drug problem and the crisis of the homeless. These programs will soak up billions of dollars, and many years will pass before results begin to show.

It occurs to you, as you guide your car onto an expressway ramp that curves around the stadium, that if every Christian in Atlanta responded to the gospel like Louise, the city would be a very different place. You find yourself longing for more eccentrics.

Chapter 21

# Dr. Donahue's
# Crack Solutions

For the first time ever I watched an entire episode of *Donahue* on TV, and it was a classic. The topic of the day, "crack babies," followed up sensational reports in the *New York Post* and *Wall Street Journal* on yet another social problem that should terrify the American public.

First, the *Post* reporters were brought out to explain the problem. Around 4 million babies have been born to users of the drug "crack," an exceptionally potent form of cocaine. These babies, born addicted and underweight, often have severe physical and emotional problems. The oldest of these offspring are now invading the classrooms of public schools, which already have their hands full with "normal" children. Crack children have an impossibly low attention span, exhibit hostile behavior, and show few signs of a moral conscience.

In short, the U.S. is being overrun by a large group of young citizens who will further strain health and education resources, and who give every indication of eventually adding to the burdens of juvenile and adult detention centers. The reporters predicted that crack children would become the number one social problem in the U.S.

Donahue's producers had managed to persuade two crack mothers—one African-American, one white—to appear on the show, and after the *Post* reporters outlined the scope of the problem, Donahue introduced the two. Tension in the audience visibly increased. The middle-class, mostly female spectators, who had just heard that drug users were unleashing a plague on their society, now had a chance to face down in person two real-life carriers of that plague.

The white crack mother seemed on drugs at that very moment. Slumping down in her chair behind the protective shield of dark glasses, she gave slurred, sluggish responses to questions. The African-American woman, currently pregnant with her second crack baby, proved quite articulate. "I've been clean for two days now," she said. "Somebody was nice to me and showed me some respect. They put me up in a hotel room for two nights and treated me like a person, and for the first time I wanted to change. I wanted to be better. And so I didn't have to use the crack." Loud applause.

Donahue jumped in with a homily. "See, these women need compassion," he said, holding out an open hand in their direction. "We've got to get off our 'hickory stick' morality. What good will it do to punish these women?" More applause.

Then he turned to the African-American woman and asked a question that was undoubtedly lurking in the minds of most of the audience. "Now, help us out here. We're trying to understand. You had one crack baby already, right? And you saw the physical problems that child went through. Yet you got pregnant again. Why?"

She thought for a moment. "Well, all I can say is, accidents do happen," she said at last. With that, she lost her sympathetic audience. Some booed and hissed. Others shook their heads angrily. As taxpayers, they would be asked to contribute tens of billions of dollars to pay for the problems presented by crack babies. Accidents may happen—but 4 million accidents? A social worker, the final member of the panel, quickly jumped in. "The only way these women can support their habit is by prostitution, turning twenty to thirty tricks a night. In their health condition, they normally don't menstruate, and often don't notice they are pregnant until four or five months into term, too late for a legal abortion."

Judging by the comments and questions that followed, however, the audience had used up its reservoir of compassion. "Why should I have to pay for their irresponsible behavior?" asked one woman, trembling with anger. "Shouldn't they be the ones to face the consequences? And it's not just themselves they're hurting—what about all those innocent babies!"

Another suggested sterilizing any woman who delivered a crack baby. Donahue seized on her suggestion: "And should we sterilize alcohol-abusing mothers? Tobacco-abusing mothers? Should we turn the police loose to knock on doors and sniff out any mothers unfit to bear children?" The woman appeared confused, but stood by her original suggestion. Something must be done.

So what can be done? Education is the answer, said the *Post* reporters. Yes, education, echoed the social worker. The articulate crack mother nodded in agreement; the sluggish one simply nodded.

I happened to be watching the *Donahue* show in a friend's living room, sitting next to a doctor who worked in Chicago's Cook County Hospital emergency room. As Donahue's guests rallied around the suggestion of education as the fix-all, this doctor suddenly laughed aloud. "The addicts I treat educate *me* about their condition," he said. "They like to portray themselves as poor, ignorant victims, but I've found many of them can interpret the charts on blood count and other vital stats better than most health workers."

If education were the simple answer, would crack have made such inroads among the literate middle class? If education were the answer, wouldn't the pregnant woman on the panel have given up her habit after she bore her first child—or at least used a fail-safe birth control method? If education alone were the answer, smokers and alcoholics would now be extinct in America.

Alcoholics Anonymous discovered long ago that the path toward cure involves more than a quick-fix solution based on increased knowledge. In fact, it involves a change that seems more theological than educational. Somehow the "victim" of addictive behavior must regain an underlying sense of human dignity and choice, a profound reawakening that usually requires much time, attention, and love.

AA members recite their creed at every meeting, a creed that renounces the notion that any of us are helpless, ignorant victims of overwhelming forces. I am a human being, morally responsible, and the choices I make affect not only me but also my family and society all around me. I will need help—from my friends and family, from fellow abusers, from a Higher Power—but at the outset I must own my capability of moral choice.

I have long been impressed by the unique way Alcoholics Anonymous combines seeming opposites: compassion that still insists on moral responsibility; community support that somehow fosters individual dignity; self-actualization that comes from dependence on a Higher Power. It is only natural that these concepts sound like Christian theology, since AA was founded by committed Christians. But such ideas are rather difficult to communicate to a whole society—let alone to get across on Phil Donahue's show.

# Chapter 22

# Those Were the Days, My Friend

*Things fall apart; the centre cannot hold;*
*Mere anarchy is loosed upon the world,*
*The blood-dimmed tide is loosed, and everywhere*
*The ceremony of innocence is drowned;*
*The best lack all conviction, while the worst*
*Are full of passionate intensity.*

—W. B. YEATS

Just as the Depression and World War II marked an entire generation, the decade of the 1960s left its mark on their offspring. Those of us who grew up in that tumultuous decade are still dealing with its impact—all of society, in fact, is dealing with it.

I was ten when the sixties began and twenty when it ended. In some ways I passed through the decade protected by a Teflon shield of religion and subculture. I had never developed a taste for music written after 1890, and mind-altering drugs never tempted me. More, I spent the later sixties on the campus of a Christian college: while secular university students were holding college presidents hostage and bombing buildings, our most daring protesters lobbied meekly against compulsory chapel. Still, despite my isolation, I was profoundly affected by those years of discontent.

At the time, it appeared that the world was standing at a threshold. When Parisian students took to the barricades in 1968, political conservatives shrieked about the end of all civilization and the unstoppable juggernaut of communism. Christian gurus like Francis Schaeffer predicted mounting unrest that would lead to cultural anarchy. No one, absolutely no one, foretold what actually did take place over the next two decades: a withdrawal from political to personal concerns, a surge in MBA degrees, the conquests of Yuppiedom, a retreat from civil rights activism, the elections of Ronald Reagan and two George Bushes.

It became evident that the sixties represented, more than anything, a fluke of demographics. Baby boomers were one of the few generations in U.S. history larger than the generation to follow them; naturally, their rite of passage would have a disproportionate impact. The population bulge moved through adolescence and young adulthood like a small pig moving through a boa constrictor: it surely changed the shape of its surroundings but eventually, like everything else, it too was absorbed.

The sixties began with an emphasis on ideals: peace, love, community, justice, equality. A renewed emphasis on spirituality drove many high school and college students to "get high on Jesus." A passion for ideals, though, is always difficult to sustain, and gradually the focus shifted from *substance* toward *style*. American corporations jumped in, cranking out designer blue jeans and sneakers, machine-cut leather fringe, and prewashed tie-dyed T-shirts. Facial hair sprouted in unlikely places: on bankers and politicians and stockbrokers. Music groups like the Grateful Dead, which had begun as anti-establishment rebels, became billion-dollar properties.

As the ideals faded or got co-opted, what remained was an emphasis on physicality. Consider what has endured as a legacy from the sixties: an active involvement with the outdoors; music that can be felt, literally, in the body's vibrating cells; a body-consciousness expressed through meditation, tai chi, or other New Age transmutations; drugs; and, of course, the sexual revolution. All these features of our modern landscape express a heightened physicality that traces back to the sixties.

I find it ironic, and sad, that so many of the lofty ideals from the sixties have evaporated away, leaving us with mere physical emblems, for what marked me during the sixties had nothing to do with these emblems. I think back with nostalgia on the passion of that decade. Though wild and unformed, that passion was strong enough to prompt thousands of clergy and students to head south on buses and risk their lives for a cause in Mississippi and Alabama, and strong enough to inspire students to resist a war they could not support. In the sixties, people thought with their hearts more than with their heads.

> *since feeling is first*
> *who pays any attention*
> *to the syntax of things?*
> —E. E. CUMMINGS

The sixties made us question cherished national values like global power, unlimited economic growth, and conspicuous consumption. If someone inquired about career goals, you would never hear the answer, "I think I'll specialize in arbitrage, or maybe junk bond financing." The respectable response then was "social work" or "legal services for the poor." Students questioned everyday things, too, like the macho ritual of football and lusty beauty pageants.

Today, beauty pageants, football, and economic growth are all thriving. Apparently the boa constrictor has absorbed the lump. The odd thing is, many important questions raised in the sixties are now more relevant than ever. People worried about the environment back then, long before anyone had heard such phrases as "global warming" and "ozone depletion." They worried about the national debt LBJ was piling up to pay for the war in Vietnam; those amounts would barely cover a month's interest on the national debt in later years. They worried about overpopulation at a time when the brittle earth supported 2 billion *fewer* human beings. Maybe the main problem with the spirit of the sixties is that it surfaced thirty years too soon.

I have a vague premonition that we haven't seen the end of convulsive protest. Perhaps the youth of this century will resume marching in the streets, in protest against the monstrous national debt we've bequeathed them and the polluted, overcrowded, soil-depleted, clear-cut, strip-mined planet we've left behind. And, who knows, we oldsters who grew up during the sixties may take to the streets again as well. I have a hunch that if we do so, next time around we will be agitating for increased Social Security benefits, health care, and other legislative largesse we've come to call "entitlements."

# Chapter 23

# Health and the God Factor

When Dr. David Larson was training for a career in psychiatry, faculty advisers warned him, "You'll harm your patients if you try to combine your Christian faith with the practice of psychiatry. It's clinically impossible." Instructors insisted that religion usually harms a person's mental health.

Does research confirm that notion? Larson wondered. Or is it a myth passed around in academic circles? His curiosity led him on a quest he followed for fifteen years, until his untimely death in 2002 at the age of fifty-four. He spent much of his time poring over academic journals and obscure research reports, pondering "negative curvilinear variables" and other data, seeking clues into how religion affects mental and physical health.

Right away Larson noticed that most research studies ignored the subject of religion altogether. This seemed odd, since 90 percent of Americans believe in God, almost half attend religious services weekly, and a large minority claim religion is "very important" in their lives. Could the omission reflect the antireligious bias of the field? Less than half of psychiatrists and psychologists claim to believe in God, and one survey found that 40 percent regard organized religion as "always, or usually, psychologically harmful."

Even though modern surveys tended to avoid explicit questions on faith, Larson found that some had asked basic questions about religious involvement. He examined these findings, then broadened his search to include anything that might indicate the effect of Christian commitment on health. What he found shocked him. A sampling:

- Regular church attenders live longer. Religiousness markedly reduces the incidence of heart attack, arteriosclerosis, high blood pressure, and hypertension.
- Religious people are less likely to abuse alcohol and far less likely to use illicit drugs. Conversely, one study found that 89 percent of alcoholics had lost interest in religion during their teenage years.
- Prison inmates who make a religious commitment are less likely than their counterparts to return to jail after release.
- Marital satisfaction and overall well-being tend to increase with church attendance; depression rates decline.
- Religious commitment offers some protection against one of the nation's greatest health problems: divorce. People who attend church regularly are more than twice as likely to remain married.

Protection against divorce is important for the following reasons:

- Divorce dramatically increases the likelihood of early death from stroke, hypertension, respiratory cancer, and intestinal cancer. Astonishingly, being divorced and a nonsmoker is only slightly less dangerous than smoking a pack or more a day and staying married! (Should divorce summons papers come with a surgeon general's warning, too?)

- Divorce also disrupts mental health, especially for men. The suicide rate for white males goes up by a factor of four with divorce, and they have ten times the probability of needing psychiatric care.
- Divorce takes a devastating toll on children. Proportionately twice as many criminals come from single-parent homes. Indeed, family structure proves more effective than economic status in predicting a life in crime. Children from broken homes are more likely to do poorly in school, abuse drugs, and attempt suicide.

In short, Larson found that religious commitment, far from causing health problems, has a pronounced effect on reducing them. "In essence the studies empirically verify the wisdom of the book of Proverbs," he concluded. "Those who follow biblical values live longer, enjoy life more, and are less diseased. The facts are in; we need to get the word out." As a consultant to the National Institutes of Health and a fellow of the newly formed Paul Tournier Institute (sponsored by the Christian Medical and Dental Society), he sought to do just that.

Dr. Larson, who lived near Washington, D.C., believed such facts should influence public policy. "Decision makers can't be expected to write laws that reflect biblical values, but I've found they do respond to two things: 1) staying alive and 2) saving money. We know beyond doubt that divorce, for example, hurts all parties and costs society dearly—shouldn't public policy somehow favor stable marriages?"

Larson's researchers point out that the key factor is the degree of religious commitment, not any particular affiliation. Dedicated Mormons, Jews, Catholics, and Protestants all manifest improved health. The psychoanalyst Carl Jung wrote: "I have treated many hundreds of patients, the larger number being Protestants, a smaller number Jews and not more than five or six believing Catholics. Among all my patients in the second half of my life . . . there has not been one whose problem in the last resort was not that of finding a religious outlook on life. It is safe to say that every one of them fell ill because he lost that which the living religions of every age have given their followers and none of them has really been healed who did not regain his religious outlook."

According to Larson, it would be difficult to concoct a better recipe for health than the nine-word prescription given in Galatians 5: love, joy, peace, patience, kindness, goodness, faithfulness, gentleness, and self-control. Paul playfully comments, "Against such things there is no law." In view of Larson's findings, perhaps we should add a footnote, "To promote such things there should be a law."

I have my doubts whether any amount of empirical data will persuade the U.S. Congress to enact legislation along the lines Larson's research suggests. As a nation, we seem far more interested in preserving the right to destroy ourselves. However, the findings do hint at an approach that may prove useful to the church in the twenty-first century.

In the not-so-distant past the American church and state recognized many of the same values: sacredness and dignity of human life, sexual fidelity, family stability, discipline, moderation. Increasingly, those values have been drifting apart, and the church may not be able to stop that trend in a secularized society. But we can strive to fulfill Jesus' original challenge: to serve as the salt of the earth, the light of the world, a city on a hill.

Although we may not convert the whole hill, we need not be

ashamed of erecting a different kind of city on the landscape of our troubled planet. As the research clearly shows, what is "good" in the moral sense, in the city of God, is also good in the pragmatic sense, in the city of man. To paraphrase John Locke, Christianity makes sense in this world as well as in the next.

# Chapter 24

# Shakespeare and
# the Politicians

In a moment of idealism, I made a New Year's resolution to read all thirty-eight of Shakespeare's plays in one year. Five years passed before I completed my goal, yet to my surprise fulfilling the task seemed far more like entertainment than like work. I always looked forward to the designated Shakespeare evening, finding the plays to be unfailingly witty and profound, and oddly up-to-date.

Once, with CNN playing softly in the background, I decided to reflect on what I had learned. "Love cools, friendship falls off, brothers divide; in cities, mutinies, in countries, discord; in palaces, treason; and the bond cracked twixt son and father." Those words from *King Lear* sounded suspiciously like commentators describing the modern world. Too bleak for most generations' taste, *King Lear* was performed for centuries in a happy-ending version. Now that modern sensibilities have caught up with its dark vision, it has become Shakespeare's most revered play.

"Each new morn new widows howl, new orphans cry, new sorrows strike heaven on the face"—was that *Macbeth* or Jesse Jackson? Shakespeare's depictions of crime, injustice, war, treachery, and greed demonstrate that, no matter what either political party says, these problems are not mutations in America of the 1990s; they have been around since Eden.

Some major differences between the Elizabethan view of the world and our own stood out as well. Listening to politicians from both parties, I get the distinct notion that if we could just keep the economy rolling, defeat terrorism, and educate all those misguided kids in gangs, why then a golden age would return to America. Social problems (the closest modern equivalent to "evil") trace back to poverty and lack of education.

Shakespeare would disagree. "They are as sick that surfeit with too much as they that starve with nothing," observed the maid of an heiress in *Merchant of Venice*. Shakespeare showed genuine respect for the decency of the lower classes. The real villains were rich and powerful, people like Macbeth and Richard III who had every advantage of education, wealth, and fine breeding. I am struck that many greats in literature—Shakespeare, Tolstoy, Balzac, Dickens—scoff at the idea that poverty lies at the root of evil. For them, evil raises its ugly head most monstrously within the upper classes.

*King Lear* states it best: "Through tattered clothes small vices do appear; robes and furred gowns hide all. Plate sin with gold. . . ." Lear learned this lesson the hard way. Cast out of his own castle by his avaricious daughters, he wandered alone through a terrific rainstorm, finally taking shelter in a cave with a refugee. The experience revealed to him a "theology of reversal," and for the first time he understood the plight of the poor and homeless:

*Poor naked wretches, wheresoe'r you are,*
*That bide the pelting of this pitiless storm,*

*How shall your houseless heads and unfed sides,*
*Your looped and windowed raggedness, defend you*
*From seasons such as these? O, I have ta'en*
*Too little care of this! Take physic, pomp;*
*Expose thyself to feel what wretches feel,*
*That thou mayst shake the superflux to them*
*And show the heavens more just.*

It is not the only scene in *Lear* that rings with overtones of the Incarnation of Jesus.


Republicans blame a Democratic administration for society's ills while Democrats blame a Republican Congress—or vice versa, depending on the decade. Shakespeare's characters are as likely to implicate God. "Wilt thou, O God, fly from such gentle lambs and throw them in the entrails of the wolf? When didst thou sleep when such a deed was done?" cries one after a murderous crime. "O God, seest Thou this, and bearest so long?" laments another.

These anguished cries ironically reveal a belief in Providence that underlies all of Shakespeare's plays. You rail against God only if you still believe God is active. As seen most clearly in the multiplay cycle centering on Henry VI, for Shakespeare history involved more than the rise and fall of rulers and nations. The turmoil and civil strife in England signified God's judgment. This is a harsh message, one I never hear on CNN.

In Shakespeare's time, people still lived out their days under the shadow of divine reward and punishment, an assumption that tends to put boundaries around evil. In *Richard III,* a hired assassin trembles before his assignment, fearing "Not to kill him, having a warrant, but to be damned for killing him, from the which no warrant can defend me." And in *Henry VI* the Earl of Warwick prays, ". . . ere my knee rise from the earth's cold face, I throw my hands, mine eyes, my heart to Thee, Thou setter-up and plucker-down of kings . . ." Our leaders could use a dose of such humility.

One last irony struck me as I pondered the Elizabethan era and our own. Comparing Shakespeare's characters with modern-day politicians, I could not help thinking how we as men and women have shrunk. The "politics of marginalization" rules in the USA. Rioters riot because they can't help it, teens get pregnant because their drives overpower them, "pro-choice" women choose abortion because they "have no choice." The message is clear: we are products of our genes, our families, and our cultures, nothing more.

In contrast, the characters in Shakespeare stride like giants across the stage. I find it wonderfully refreshing to read of people who have a sense of personal *destiny* about them. These are not automatons or victims, but free individuals making choices, some malignant and some noble. As the master playwright insists, they must then live with the consequences. Lady Macbeth hoped otherwise: "A little water clears us of this deed," she said as she and her husband rinsed their hands of blood. How wrong she was.

Lady Macbeth died haunted by guilt, and her husband mourned her with these eloquent words of despair:

*Life's but a walking shadow, a poor player*
*That struts and frets his hour upon the stage*
*And then is heard no more. It is a tale*
*Told by an idiot, full of sound and fury,*
*Signifying nothing.*

Shakespeare's plays alone offer enough evidence to refute that nihilism. As the Victorian scholar A. C. Bradley wrote, in words that apply to almost all of Shakespeare's characters, "No one ever closes a tragedy with the feeling that man is a poor mean creature. He may be wretched and he may be awful but he is not small." It's enough to make you nostalgic.

Chapter 25

# Whatever Happened
# to Deism?

The salvation of this human world lies nowhere else than in the human heart. . . . The only backbone to our actions, if they are to be moral, is responsibility. Responsibility to something higher than my family, my firm, my country, my success—responsibility to the order of being where all our actions are indelibly recorded and where, and only where, they will be properly judged."

Those words, addressed to the U.S. Congress, came not from Billy Graham or Pat Robertson, but from Vaclav Havel, then president of one of the least religious countries on earth, the Czech Republic.

When the Library of Congress invited Havel to serve as guest editor of its magazine *Civilization*, he devoted the issue to the need for religious foundations, concluding, "I have become increasingly convinced that the crisis of the much-needed global responsibility is in principle due to the fact that we have lost the certainty that the Universe, nature, existence and our lives are the work of creation guided by a definite intention, that it has a definite meaning and follows a definite purpose." He warned that modern Western civilization is "the first atheistic civilization in the history of humankind."

The letters section of the next issue included a chorus of outcries. How could an intellectual like Havel call for a return to religion? Doesn't he know that religion gives rise to violence, racism, censorship, and intolerance? Havel could do so, of course, because he had lived under an atheistic regime that outdid any misguided religion in those categories.

Havel does not call himself a Christian, for he rightly understands that to do so would require acknowledging Jesus as an incarnation of God. His theology remains vague, akin to classical deism: God created the world, then entrusted it to us, requiring only that we accept our role as subject to the higher order.

Havel's pronouncements on religion—prophetic at times, nebulous at others—bring to mind the sweeping analysis of another intellectual earlier in this century. Indeed, Havel's diagnosis of the moral rot in modern society borrows heavily from T. S. Eliot. Like Havel, Eliot faced a world in moral turmoil. With Hitler controlling Western Europe and Stalin controlling the East, Eliot turned to Christianity reluctantly, as the only force capable of fighting those demons.

Along the way, though, Eliot gained the faith that Havel thus far lacks. He said, "I take for granted that Christian revelation is the only full revelation and that the fullness of Christian revelation resides in the essential fact of the Incarnation. . . . The division between those who accept, and those who deny, Christian revelation I take to be the most profound division between human beings."

Some accused Eliot of embracing Christianity for utilitarian reasons, because the world needed it. He protested. "What is worst of all is to advocate Christianity, not because it is true, but because it might be beneficial," he said. "To justify Christianity because it provides a foundation of morality, instead of showing the necessity of Christian morality from the truth of Christianity, is a very dangerous diversion."

The issue of *Civilization* edited by Havel contained a report on an exhibition opening at the Library of Congress, "Religion and the Founding of the American Republic." One of its displays featured a report by a man who encountered President Thomas Jefferson on his way to church, carrying a large red prayer book. The friend asked why Jefferson would attend church, since he did not believe a word of it. Jefferson replied, "Sir, no nation has ever yet existed or been governed without religion. Nor can be. The Christian religion is the best religion that has been given to man and I as chief Magistrate of this nation am bound to give it the sanction of my example." (Jefferson, the exhibit noted, attended church every Sunday during his presidency—a church that met in the House of Representatives!)

Listening to Havel, hearing in his words sentiments like those held by Thomas Jefferson and Benjamin Franklin, I am reminded of a mystery of religious history. Havel appears to promote a most respectable deism that preserves the high standards of religion while eliminating some of its excesses. Whatever happened to deism?

Despite being supported by the leading intellects of the American Revolution, despite being based on the best reason and science of its day, deism virtually disappeared from the scene by 1810, even before Jefferson's death.

Unlike Vaclav Havel, I have little faith that a new breed of rational deists will arise to restore a form of global order and morality. I conclude that deism failed, and will always fail, because of its conception of God. A few intellectuals may enjoy worshiping an absentee landlord, but most Christians prefer Jesus' notion of God as a loving father. We need more than a mere watchmaker who winds up the universe and lets it tick. We need love, and mercy, and forgiveness, and grace—qualities only a personal God can offer.

T. S. Eliot understood the contrast clearly: "To me, religion has brought at least the perception of something above morals, and therefore extremely terrifying; it has brought me not happiness, but the sense of something above happiness and therefore more terrifying than ordinary pain and misery: the very dark night and the desert . . . I had far rather walk, as I do, in daily terror of eternity, than feel that this was only a children's game in which all the contestants would get equally worthless prizes in the end."

# Chapter 26

# Could It Happen Here?

Henri Nouwen wrote with a tone of melancholy about return visits to his boyhood home in the Netherlands, where in one generation vibrant Catholicism had faded into a quaint ritual. A few months before his death, he spoke to a paltry crowd of thirty-six students at the seminary he had attended at a time when it bustled with hundreds of eager candidates for priesthood.

Nouwen's own devout family had rejoiced in his choice of vocation, though many in the family later lost interest. He might be called on to christen a niece or nephew, but mostly he was seen as a cultural relic. "I feel like an entertainer who is far from entertaining," he said after one such event.

On a visit to the Low Countries, I encountered many reminders of the abrupt decline in European faith. Dutch Christians told me that a century ago, 98 percent of all Dutch people attended church regularly; within two generations the percentage fell into the low teens. Almost half the church buildings in Holland have been destroyed or converted into restaurants, art galleries, or condominiums.

I attended a vespers service in Brussels, Belgium, in a church renowned for its stained glass. Ten of us sat under the high Gothic arches, my wife and I the only ones under the age of seventy. Outside, far more tourists stood in line complaining about the sign announcing the church's closure to tourists during the service. For a majority of Europeans, the church seems wholly irrelevant.

A German correspondent wrote me about Europeans' reaction to Islamic terrorism. Newspapers there voice thoughts like this: *Muslim fanatics are willing to die for their God; we no longer even believe in God. What do we have as an alternative?* I sensed some of the same existential anxiety in the Netherlands. Muslims have a more pronounced and visible presence in Western Europe than in the United States, and xenophobic movements in Germany, Spain, Austria, and France have fed on the resulting anxieties.

Holland is now requiring new citizens to be proficient in the Dutch language and know something of Dutch culture. Yet once again Europeans ask themselves, What does our culture offer as an alternative? The new European Union constitution barely acknowledges the continent's Christian heritage.

My hosts in the Netherlands look to the United States as a model of a modern nation that maintains a vital religious faith. Whenever I visit Europe, though, and see the mostly hollow shells of an institution that dominated the continent for fifteen hundred years, I wonder if the same pattern will play out here. Will the decline of faith that A. N. Wilson, himself one of its symbols, documented in the book *God's Funeral* occur in the United States?

Wilson writes, "God's funeral was not, as many in the nineteenth century might have thought, the end of a phase of human intellectual history. It was the withdrawal of a great Love-object." Wilson admits a deep loss in at least two areas. For the first time in history, many people no longer feel the need to pray or worship. Also uniquely, many see no world of value outside ourselves, no objective transcendent truth. Human beings alone must define values and meaning—and if the previous century offers any indication of the result, we face a bleak future indeed.

I have some hope that the United States will not go the way of Western Europe. In the first place, we have strong seminaries and Christian colleges that may help future generations resist the avalanche of disbelief that swept across Europe. Perhaps more important, the U.S. church has long been a mission-sending church. (Sometimes I wonder if God continues to bless our nation, despite its decadence, for this reason alone.)

American Christians trained in Enlightenment reductionism can learn about spiritual warfare firsthand on mission trips to South America. We can learn about suffering from the church in China, about passionate evangelism from Africa, and about intercessory prayer from Korea. Just as nothing threatens my faith like a visit to agnostic Europe, nothing invigorates my faith more than a visit to churches in non-Western countries.

Perhaps we have not heard the last from the church in Europe either. I met with Paul Nouwen, Henri's younger brother, who as head of the Dutch equivalent of the American Automobile Association oversaw services to some 6 million members. After Henri's unexpected death at sixty-four in 1996, Paul stood before a gathering of diplomats, ambassadors, members of Parliament, and other dignitaries. He told of sitting at Henri's funeral and hearing people from many countries speak of Henri's impact on their lives.

"I realized that compared to Henri, I have nothing," he said. "And as I sat there listening, the difference became clear—Henri had God. That made all the difference." In a humble spirit, Paul

Nouwen proceeded to tell of the changes he was making, to better prepare for his own death and restore a relationship with the God whom his brother knew so well. As his brother testified, Henri, who had lived as a missionary in North and South America, ended up as a missionary back in his heartsick homeland.

# Chapter 27

# Running Away from Fugitives

I just have the feeling the country's headed in the wrong direction," said one friend of mine. Many people share her uneasiness. Violent crime has increased 560 percent since the 1960s. Promiscuity—in sex, in drugs, in violence, in consumption—has become the spirit of the age. The United States can be considered a Christian nation only in the loosest sense of the term. "God will turn his back on America," said my friend, shaking her head sadly.

All this concern about "the decline of America" got me wondering how much attention God pays to national boundaries. Does God really judge the United States or any other country *as a national entity?* I have often heard this verse quoted as a formula for national revival: "If my people, who are called by my name, will humble themselves and pray and seek my face and turn from their wicked ways, then will I hear from heaven and will forgive their sin and will heal their land" (2 Chronicles 7:14). Yet that promise was given as part of God's covenant relationship with the ancient Hebrews on the occasion of the dedication of Solomon's temple, God's dwelling place on earth. Have we any reason to assume God has a similar covenant arrangement with the USA?

Certainly the Old Testament shows God dealing with national entities: the prophets called down judgment on Israel and Judah as well as Philistia, Assyria, and Babylon. But the New Testament seems to introduce a major shift: God is now working not primarily through nations, but through an invisible kingdom that transcends nations. Jesus stressed "the kingdom of Heaven" as the central focus of God's activity on earth, a kingdom that permeates society so as to gradually affect the whole, like salt sprinkled on meat.

As I now reflect on Jesus' stories of the kingdom, I sense that much uneasiness among Christians today stems from a confusion of the two kingdoms, visible and invisible. Each time an election rolls around, Christians debate whether this or that candidate is "God's man" for the White House. Projecting myself back into Jesus' time, I have difficulty imagining him pondering whether Tiberius, Octavius, or Julius Caesar—not to mention Nero or Caligula—was "God's man" for the empire. What took place in Rome was on another plane entirely from the kingdom of God.

The apostle Paul cared deeply about individual churches in Galatia, Ephesus, Corinth, and Rome, but I find no indication that he gave any thought to a "Christianized" Roman Empire. The Book of Revelation continues the pattern: that book records specific messages to seven churches but dismisses the political entity of Rome as "Babylon the great the mother of prostitutes and of the abominations of the earth."

Some historians argue that the church loses sight of its original mission as it moves closer to the seat of power. Witness the era of Constantine, and the Dark Ages, and Europe just before the Reformation. We may be seeing history repeat itself. The church has faced the constant temptation of becoming the "morals police" of society.

In 1991, as communism fell in Poland, 70 percent of Poles approved of the Catholic Church as a moral and spiritual force. Now only 40 percent approve, mainly because of its "interference" in politics. Modern Poland does not practice church-state separation: a new media law says radio and TV broadcasts must "respect the Christian system of values," and the state funds the teaching of Catholicism in Polish public schools. Yet the new coziness between church and government has resulted in a loss of respect for the church.

At various points in U.S. history (the 1850s, the time of Prohibition, and most recently during the Moral Majority movement of the 1980s), the Christian church has marked an ascendancy into politics. Now, it appears, the church and politics may be heading in different directions. The more I understand Jesus' message of the kingdom of God, the less alarm I feel over that trend. Our real challenge, the focus of our energy, should not be to Christianize the United States (always a losing battle) but rather to strive to be Christ's church in an increasingly hostile world. As Karl Barth said, "[The church] exists . . . to set up in the world a new sign which is radically dissimilar to [the world's] own manner and which contradicts it in a way which is full of promise."

Ironically, if indeed the United States is sliding down a slippery moral slope, that may better allow the church to set up "a new sign . . . which is full of promise." Already I see some evidence of that trend. Magazine writers, sociologists, and hostile politicians have all had to agree about the grievously harmful effects of single-parent families. Meanwhile, sociologist Robert Bellah, after interviewing hundreds of married couples, identified evangelical Christians as the only group that could articulate a reason for marriage commitments that went beyond selfish interests. Research such as that uncovered by Dr. David Larson increasingly supports the healthy side benefits of a life of faith.

"In a world of fugitives," said T. S. Eliot, "the person taking the opposite direction will appear to run away." As America slides, I will work and pray for the kingdom of God to advance. If the gates of Hell cannot prevail against the church, the contemporary political scene hardly offers much threat.

Part Five

✠

Finding

God

Among

the

Headlines

Chapter 28

# Russia's Untold Story

A ll history, once you strip the rind off the kernel, is really spiritual," wrote historian Arnold Toynbee. The events in the former Soviet Union demonstrate the truth of his statement. I visited there as part of a delegation of nineteen Christian leaders in the fall of 1991, just after the aborted coup that temporarily deposed Mikhail Gorbachev and just before Boris Yeltsin's ascendance to power. Wherever we went, government officials and private citizens alike affirmed that the true crisis in their nation was moral and spiritual. We heard that opinion expressed so adamantly and so often that I came to see it as the great untold story of Russia.

Almost overnight Russia moved away from an official position of atheism and hostility to become perhaps the most open mission field in the world. Wherever we went, officials invited us to set up exchange programs, relief efforts, study centers, and religious publishing ventures. The Russian leaders voiced a fear of total collapse and anarchy unless their society could find a way to change at the core. (Mainly due to lobbying by the Russian Orthodox Church, many restrictions were soon reinstated.)

After listening to a parade of politicians and government leaders follow the same script of unvarying politeness and respect for Christianity, it was easy to lose sight of how radically the nation had changed. Russian leaders seemed far more receptive to Christian influence than, say, their counterparts in the United States. Could their predecessors have been so devilish? An unexpected visit from Basil brought a jarring reminder of what life had been like for Christians under the communist regime.

For years Basil, who lived in Moldavia, had clandestinely tuned in to shortwave programs from the West. Basil first heard a news item about our delegation on Voice of America. Then, incredulous, he listened as the official national radio network gave reports of our meetings with the Parliament and the KGB. The new openness toward religion seemed so inconceivable to Basil that he got on a night train and made the fourteen-hour journey from Moldavia to Moscow in order to see us.

Basil showed up in the lobby early one morning, just as we were gathering to pray and review the day's schedule. He had broad, hulking shoulders and the rugged, weather-beaten features of a farmer, and he looked ill at ease in a suit and tie. He had a most peculiar smile: two front teeth on the top row were missing, and when he smiled, gold fillings in the back molars gleamed faintly through the gap. He presented us with sacks of gorgeous purple grapes and golden apples, which he had handpicked and carried on his lap from Moldavia. He asked for five minutes to address us.

When Basil opened his mouth and the first sound came out, I jumped. We were meeting in a small room, and Basil spoke at the decibel level of a freight train. I have never heard a louder voice from any human being. We soon learned why.

In 1962, Basil founded a small publishing company with his

own funds. He printed Christian pamphlets, distributing a total of seven hundred thousand before the KGB paid him a visit. They demanded that he stop, and when he refused, they arrested him and sent him to a labor camp. At first Basil was perplexed. Why should he be punished for serving God? What use could he be in a labor camp? But then one morning he saw in a flash that God had provided a new opportunity.

Every morning before sunup, prisoners from the labor camp had to assemble in an open space for roll call. Camp commanders insisted on strict punctuality from prisoners, but not from guards, and so thousands of prisoners stood outdoors several minutes each morning with nothing to do. Basil, who loved to preach, decided to start a church.

As he was recounting this story in the hotel room, Basil spoke louder and faster, gesturing passionately with his arms like an opera singer. Every few sentences the translator grabbed Basil's flailing arm and asked him to please slow down and lower his voice. Each time Basil apologized, looked down at the floor, and began again in a pianissimo that within three seconds crescendoed to a fortissimo. His voice had no volume control, and the reason traced back to that early morning scene in the labor camp.

Basil preached daily to a truly captive audience. Typically, he had about two minutes before the guards arrived, rarely as long as five minutes, and as a result it took up to two weeks to deliver a single sermon. He had to shout to be heard by several thousand prisoners, a strain that made him hoarse until his voice adapted. Over the years—ten years in all—of preaching outdoors to thousands, he developed the habit of speaking at top volume and breakneck speed, a habit he could never break.

Basil completed his sentence in 1972 and devoted his energies to building an unregistered church in his village. Sometimes he visited the church among the convicts and, he proudly reported, even today a community of one hundred believers still worships in that prison.

Basil's difficulties did not end with his release from prison, though. He told us of harassment by the authorities over his unregistered church, of the threats and public slanders, and repeated vandalism of the church building. Finally, after nineteen years, opposition faded away, and he had just laid the last cement block and covered the church with a roof. He had come to Moscow, he said, to thank us for all we were doing, to bring us fresh fruit from Moldavia, and to ask one of our delegation, Alex Leonovich, to speak at the dedication of his church.

"There were many years when I had no encouragement," Basil said. By now he was weeping openly and his voice cracked but did not drop one decibel. "The words of this man, Brother Leonovich, I carried in my heart. He was the one who encouraged me when my hands were tied behind my back." Basil then reached over, grabbed Alex by the shoulders, and kissed him in the Russian style once, twice, fifteen times—one for each year, he said, that he had waited for Alex to return.

"And now, such changes, I can hardly believe them," Basil said in closing. "We have been through the valley of tears. When Billy Graham came in 1959, they let him appear on a balcony but not speak. To think that you are here in Moscow, the center of unbelief, able to talk and drink tea with the leaders of our country. It is a miracle! Brothers and sisters, be bold! With your wings you are lifting up children of the Lord. Where I come from the believers are praying for you at this minute. We believe your visit will help reach our country for God. God bless you all."

Suddenly, I burned with shame. Here we were: nineteen Christian professionals who made a comfortable living from our faith sitting in one of the most luxurious hotels in Moscow. What did we know about the kind of bedrock faith needed in this nation of people who had endured such suffering? What gave us the right to represent the Basils of Russia before the president and Parliament, let alone the KGB?

We stood and prayed with Basil, and then he left. Later that day Alex Leonovich traded in his airplane ticket, incurring a huge penalty, in order to extend his stay. "How could I possibly turn down Basil's invitation?" he said. Our group went off to be feted in grand style with a banquet at the Ukrainian embassy, and we did not see Basil again until later in the evening.

I looked forward to the event scheduled for that evening, a visit to the Journalists' Club. The inordinately polite reception we were receiving in Moscow was making me nervous. I knew that an entire atheistic state had not warmed to Christianity overnight, and I longed for a dialogue of true substance. I wanted us to be challenged with hard questions about what difference Christianity could make in a country coming apart at the seams. I could count on cynical, hard-bitten journalists to render such a challenge, I thought.

I thought wrong. This is what happened at the Journalists' Club of Moscow. First we North American Christians, seated on a spotlighted stage in a small theater, introduced ourselves. The director of Prison Fellowship International, Ron Nikkel, normally taciturn, was feeling rather expansive. "Winston Churchill said you can judge a society by its prisons," he began. "By that standard, both the USSR and the U.S. are tragedies. Our prisons are awful.

"I have been in prisons all over the world, and have talked to sociologists, behaviorists, and criminal justice experts. None of them know how to get prisoners to change. But we believe—and I have seen abundant proof—that Christ can transform a person from the inside out. Jesus, himself a prisoner, was executed, but he rose again. Now many prisoners are rising again, thanks to him."

The room fell silent, and then these "cynical, hard-bitten journalists" did something I would not have predicted in a thousand years. They broke into loud, prolonged applause. These are the questions they tossed at Ron: "What is this forgiveness? How can we find it? How do you get to know God?" Later, one of the journalists told us that his profession had a special affinity for prisoners, since many had served time themselves. For many decades, prisoners had been the primary carriers of truth in a society based on lies.

Evidently, the journalistic elite of Moscow would not be the ones to challenge our basic Christian beliefs. They seemed far more intent on grasping after them, as if grasping for rare secrets of life that had been concealed for seventy years. After all of us seated onstage had introduced ourselves, the journalists themselves spoke.

A distinguished-looking, silver-haired gentleman stood first, identifying himself as an editor of the *Literary Gazette*, which we knew to be one of the most prestigious journals in Russia. "No doubt you know of the problems in our country," he said. "I tell you, however, that the greatest problem is not that we don't have enough sausages. Far worse, we don't have enough ideas. We don't know what to think. The ground has been pulled out from under us. We thank you deeply for coming to our country and holding before us morality, and hope, and faith. It is beautiful to see you in this place. You represent exactly what we need."

The next speaker was his polar opposite, a dissident who specialized in writing political satire. Slovenly dressed, ungroomed, and passionate, with a bald head but spectacular two-inch eyebrows, he looked as if he had stepped straight from a Dostoyevsky novel. This character spoke in a voice almost as loud as Basil's. He had a bad stutter—odd to hear in a foreign language—and just as he reached a climactic point he would hang up on a word. "You are our salvation, our only hope!" he shouted. "We had a lawful country, a society with religious beliefs, but that was all destroyed in seventy years. Our souls were su-su-su-sucked out. Truth was de-de-destroyed. In the last stage, which we have just lived through, even the c-c-c-c-c-communist morale was destroyed."

Next, a beautiful blond woman wearing a red silk blouse and a leather skirt and matching boots made her way to the aisle. She stood just before the stage, her hands clutching a designer purse. I had not seen such fine clothes in Moscow. My translator whispered to me that she was a popular newscaster—something like the Connie Chung or Diane Sawyer of Russia. "I am so shaken to be here tonight," she said, and then paused a moment to control her voice.

"I am shaking! I feel so blessed to learn that American leaders are concerned with spiritual and moral problems. I am a person educated in religion and yet I am only on the first step in understanding what is God. So many visitors have come here to make a profit in our country, but I am so thankful that the American intelligentsia care enough to come and meet with people at such important levels over these issues."

She was followed by others who rose to give a similarly embarrassing overassessment of our importance as a delegation. As in previous meetings, we tried to mention flaws in American society and in the American church, but the journalists seemed altogether disinterested in apologies or critiques. They seemed, rather, starved—grievously starved for hope.

I thought of the reception our group might get at the Press Club in Washington, D.C., the questions we might prompt from the editors of the *New Republic* or *Esquire*. I tried to imagine Connie Chung or Barbara Walters being vulnerable before her peers, as this blond woman had been. As I was mulling over these thoughts, I noticed in the audience a familiar figure in a funny green suit.

The theater lights had been dimmed for our introductions, but now that the audience was responding, other lights were switched on. Sitting in the back row was Basil, he of the foghorn voice and the two-minute church in the gulag. From then on I kept one eye on Basil, wondering how an ex-convict from Moldavia felt in such an environment, among the celebrities of Moscow.

Whenever someone mentioned the word "God" or "Jesus," Basil raised both fists over his head, and even from the stage I could almost see the gleam in the gap between his teeth. On the back row, out of view of the audience, Basil was acting as our one-person charismatic cheerleading crew.

For the first time that day I glimpsed our group as Basil saw us: his ambassadors, going where he would not be invited, speaking words he could not always follow, opening doors he had thought were sealed shut forever. We, too, those of us who felt so unworthy in his presence that morning, had a role to play. It was to do our part to help guarantee that Basil stay free to worship, inside or outside the camp.

Basil stood for millions of Russian Christians who had lived out their faith in fear and trembling. Incredibly, the tables had turned. Now the journalists of Moscow applauded when they heard stories of converted prisoners, and craved news about God as a dying patient craves a miracle cure. They hung on our words about Christianity as Russian economists hung on words about capitalism, as if we were smuggling in a secret formula from the West that might salvage their land.

We were not bringing imports from the West, however. The God we served had been in Russia all along, worshiped hungrily in the camps and in the unregistered house churches and in the cathedrals the communists had not razed.

These journalists, all masters of Moscow's cocktail party circuit, had never met a simple saint like Basil. It was our job, quite simply, to introduce them.

The day after our meeting with the journalists, a direct and challenging confrontation with Marxist ideology finally came our way, on a visit to the Academy of Social Sciences. The name is misleading: until the August coup the academy functioned as the preeminent finishing school for Marxist-Leninist leaders.

Raisa Gorbachev once taught there, and many world leaders from the former socialist bloc have studied at this elite school.

Like everything else in Russia, the academy was undergoing tumultuous change. Until the fall of 1991 it received generous funding from the Communist Party, but shortly before our visit subsidies were abruptly cut off. The academy's professors, once coddled and privileged, now literally had no idea where their next paychecks would come from. In its scramble to survive, the Academy of Social Sciences was reaching out to Christians, who still had some credibility with a restive populace. The academy was even negotiating to establish a department for the study of Christianity.

Of all people in Russia, these academy professors were true believers. Fed communist theory practically from birth, they had devoted their lives to the propagation of it. One could still see relics of that intense devotion in the quasi-religious signs posted around Russia: LENIN LIVED. LENIN LIVES. LENIN WILL LIVE. They were not prepared to substitute Jesus for Lenin.

The professors recognized they had lost, perhaps forever, the battle of ideas. The cherished Marxist dream was over. Freedom scared them, and yet they could not deny its benefits. One historian present mentioned the two streams that can issue from a common source of revolution: one leads to free arrangements among citizens, the other leads to absolute power.

"We started with common ideals," he said. "Leaders of both our societies talked about justice and equality and individual rights. Yet somehow you have produced a society that with all its problems still conveys courtesy and civility. Your minorities protest against discrimination—but they do not secede or start civil wars. Somehow, beginning from similar ideals, we here have produced a society of beasts. We have murdered our own citizens in the name of the state. We know that we must move toward liberal democracy, but we don't know how. We no longer know what values to build a society upon."

Most groups we had met with plied us eagerly with questions. The academy professors seemed more anxious to talk. Listening to them, I felt I was in a political therapy session, nodding my head sympathetically as neurotic clients let long-suppressed anxieties spill out.

In the midst of this genteel discussion, one of the Marxist professors, a specialist in philosophy, rose to his feet and asked for the floor (all other speakers had remained seated). Blotches of red appeared on his face, and as soon as he began speaking, anger gushed forth. Others in the room looked around anxiously, concerned that he was straying from the mannerly dialogue. But there was no stopping this man. He had come to deliver a speech—a diatribe, really—not to fraternize with the enemy.

"We need not have God to have morality!" he said. "Erich Fromm developed a fine morality based on Man with a capital 'M.' God is not necessary. Why pretend there is a God?"

The philosopher's volume rose and his face grew even more flushed. He punctuated the air with his finger as he made each point, and I thought of the paintings of Lenin addressing the workers. I thought too of stump preachers in the South, where I had grown up. Of course! This man was a fanatic evangelist, the last true-blue, dyed-in-the-wool Marxist in Moscow. He was out to gain converts, and it mattered not at all if he was the last person in the world to believe these things. He was a bitter, wounded atheist, and he seized the chance to strike back.

"Marxism has not failed!" he shouted. "Yes, Stalin made mistakes. Yes, even our beloved Lenin made mistakes. Perhaps even Marx made mistakes. But go back to the young Marx, not the old Marx. There you will find the purity of the socialist vision. There you will find a morality based on Man with the capital 'M.' That is what we need. As for Christianity, we already tried that in Russia—for one thousand years we tried it."

We members of the delegation were fidgeting in our seats. Being yelled at by a fanatic is not a pleasant sensation, I realized, and tucked away the thought for further reflection. A few members of our group were whispering to their seatmates, and still others were clearing their throats, ready to jump in with a rebuttal.

The philosopher went on for ten or fifteen minutes until finally the emcee forced him to stop. I sensed in the atmosphere of the room an odd mixture of revenge and embarrassment. The professors waited for our response, and I cringed at the possibilities. Some of us weren't far removed from stump preachers ourselves, I knew, and the last thing the academy needed was a wounded evangelical doing battle with a wounded atheist. By the providence of God, it was Kent Hill who got the floor.

Kent Hill looks more professorial than the professors. He wears glasses, has a scholarly demeanor, and speaks in soft, measured tones, the epitome of rational discourse. He also has a PhD in Russian studies, and had taught at one university and served as president of another before taking a position at the U.S. State Department. I did not envy him the spotlight he had just stepped into, but I could not imagine a finer representative to respond on our behalf.

"First, I want to affirm your right to your beliefs," Kent began, and waited respectfully for his Russian translator. "I am concerned about intolerance in Russia today—intolerance of atheists. I recently learned of an incident where a group allowed a Christian believer to speak, but shouted down an atheist. We have not come in that spirit. We support freedom of religion, and that includes freedom for those who do not believe in God."

Tension rushed from the room as if someone had opened an air lock. The professors nodded approval, and even the philosopher gave a curt nod. Kent continued.

"The issues you have raised tonight, sir, are important issues. In fact, I cannot think of more important issues to discuss. You have touched on questions of ultimate meaning for humanity and for the universe. Our group has thought long and hard about these questions. We have reached some conclusions, and we would love to discuss those with you.

"But one night's discussion would hardly do justice to these issues. I do not feel comfortable presenting a brief response. Could I make a suggestion? My family and I are moving to Moscow in December, and I will be teaching a course in Christian Apologetics at Moscow State University. I will gladly return to your academy with Christian friends and set up a forum in which we can consider these important matters."

Again, nods of approval all around. Kent resumed, "But since I have the floor, I would like to mention why I believe the way I do." At this point, Kent shocked everyone by lapsing into fluent Russian. The professors removed their headphones and now we Americans were the ones listening to the simultaneous translation.

Kent told of a time of doubt in his life when he was tempted to abandon his Christian beliefs. He began reading Dostoyevsky's great novel *The Brothers Karamazov*—at this mention, more nods—which deals with many of the issues raised by the academy philosopher.

"At first I found myself attracted to Ivan, the agnostic. His arguments against God were powerful, especially those concerning the problem of evil. I sensed in him a sincerity and a brilliant mind. As I read Dostoyevsky's book, I found myself gradually losing faith. But to my surprise, I was eventually won over by the love shown by Ivan's brother Alyosha. Ivan had fine arguments, but he had no love. He could reason his way to a morality, but he could not create the love necessary to fulfill it. Eventually, I came to believe in Christ because I found in Him a source for that love."

With that, Kent Hill sat down, and our meeting with the Academy of Social Sciences was transformed.

It occurred to me as we drove away from the ghostly marble buildings that Kent Hill had done far more than defuse one awkward confrontation. He had given us a model of evangelism for Russia, perhaps the only model that will authentically work. First, he had begun with a genuine respect for the Russian's own beliefs, even those diametrically opposed to his own. Unlike the philosophy professor, he had listened with courtesy and compassion before speaking. Next, by moving to Moscow, Kent had committed himself to incarnational ministry. By themselves, no delegations of foreigners visiting for a week or a month will bring long-term change to the country. But a sprinkling of dedicated people who share the hardships and the turmoil, people willing to stand in the Moscow breadlines, could perhaps become the salt that savors the whole society.

Finally, Kent pointed to the source of truth latent in the Russian culture itself. His lapse into the Russian language, almost instinctive as his response turned personal, and his reference to Dostoyevsky communicated far more to that audience than if he had quoted an entire epistle from the New Testament.

It was also through reading Dostoyevsky, Solzhenitsyn reports, that he first began to understand the primacy of the spiritual over the material. That led the way to a conversion experience in a labor camp that changed the course of his life and ultimately affected the course of his nation. Solzhenitsyn too became a directional signal pointing the way back toward God. As Kent Hill had so gently revealed, the seeds of renewal already lay in Russian soil.

In *Crime and Punishment*, Dostoyevsky writes of the perilous sensation of living on one square yard of a cliff, on a narrow ledge where two feet can hardly stand, surrounded on all sides by an abyss, the ocean, everlasting darkness, everlasting solitude, and an everlasting storm. A good image for modern Russia, I decided. Everyone knows the danger on all sides; no one knows how to get off the cliff.

What went wrong in the former Soviet Union? The news media focuses on a fatally flawed economic system. Curiously, I have not seen one mention in the media of what every Russian leader insisted to us: the grave crisis is not economic or political, but rather moral and spiritual. The failure of Marxism, we were told again and again, is above all a *theological* failure.

In his Templeton Prize Address in 1983, Alexander Solzhenitsyn said, "Over half a century ago, while I was still a child, I recall hearing a number of older people offer the following explanation for the great disasters that had befallen Russia: 'Men have forgotten God; that's why all this has happened.' Since then I have spent well-nigh fifty years working on the history of our revolution; in the process I have read hundreds of books, collected hundreds of personal testimonies, and have already contributed eight volumes of my own toward the effort of clearing away the rubble left by that upheaval. But if I were asked today to formulate as concisely as possible the main cause of the ruinous revolution that swallowed up some 60 million of our people, I could not put it more accurately than to repeat: 'Men have forgotten God; that's why all this has happened.' "

Solzhenitsyn went on to say, "I myself see Christianity today as the only living spiritual force capable of undertaking the spiritual healing of Russia." When he made those remarks, the USSR was still a superpower, and Solzhenitsyn was widely assailed for his old-fashioned views. Now, less than a decade later, our delegation heard almost the identical assessment from top leaders of the nation. Above any other nation, the Soviet Union endeavored to get along without God. "Religion will disappear," Marx flatly predicted, its quaint beliefs made obsolete by the New Socialist Man. But religion did not disappear, and no New Socialist Man emerged.

In the twentieth century a morality play was conducted on a grand scale, with catastrophic consequences. What lies ahead? On the airplane on the way home, various members of our delegation tried to speculate. We all sensed the enormity of change that has already come. The new openness toward religion exceeded what any of us might have hoped for. In that regard, the prayers of millions of Christians both inside and outside Russia have been answered.

I too sensed the epic, and yet I confess that I tend toward realism, and hope does not come easily for me. I can hardly envision what a restored, much less redeemed, Russia would look like.

One thing only gives me hope. I will never forget the expressions on the faces of Basil, and the blond television newscaster, and even the vice-chairman of the KGB. Jesus' parables about the kingdom and the fig tree and the great banquet make one truth explicit: God goes where he is wanted. He does not force himself on an individual or on a nation, whether it be first-century Jews or twenty-first-century Americans. And as I look back on my visit to Russia, one impression lingers above all others: never in my life have I been among people with a more ravenous appetite for God.

Chapter 29

# The God That Failed

After my trip to Russia, I thought much about the Marxist experiment that Russians now call "seventy-four years on the road to nowhere." Why did it fail so badly? Perhaps the best answer to that question came during a meeting between our group of Christians and the editors of *Pravda*, formerly the official mouthpiece of the Communist Party.

One sample quotation from *Pravda* in 1950 shows how the newspaper got its reputation as a propaganda organ: "If you meet with difficulties in your work, or suddenly doubt your abilities, think of him—of Stalin—and you will find the confidence you need. If you feel tired in an hour when you should not, think of him—of Stalin—and your work will go well. If you are seeking a correct decision, think of him—of Stalin—and you will find that decision."

The Russians used to have a cynical saying about their two largest newspapers: "There is no *pravda* [truth] in *Izvestia* [news] and no *izvestia* in *Pravda*." After 1989, like everything else in Russia, *Pravda* underwent tumultuous change. For a time Boris Yeltsin shut it down. When I visited, in the fall of 1991, circulation figures were in a tailspin that signified communism's fall from grace: daily circulation had declined from 11 million to 700,000.

The editors of *Pravda* seemed earnest, sincere, searching—and shaken to the core. So shaken that they were now asking for help from emissaries of a religion their founder had scorned as "the opiate of the people." The editors remarked wistfully that Christianity and communism have many of the same ideals: equality, sharing, justice, and racial harmony. Yet they had to admit that the Marxist pursuit of that vision had produced the worst nightmares the world has ever seen. Why?

Sociologists, philosophers, and economists will no doubt pronounce their own postmortems over Marxism, but what struck me during the ensuing discussion is that communism failed because of two basic errors in what theologians call *anthropology*, or "the doctrine of humanity."

First, communists ignored our fallen nature. Early communists had promised the emergence of a new breed of human being, the New Socialist Man. Leon Trotsky wrote in 1924, "Man will become immeasurably stronger, wiser and subtler; his body will become more harmonized, his movements more rhythmic, his voice more musical. The forms of life will become dynamically dramatic. The average human type will rise to the heights of an Aristotle, a Goethe or a Marx. And above this ridge new peaks will rise." Today, any Russian would laugh out loud at Trotsky's prediction.

Classical Marxists fought fiercely against religion for a shrewd reason: in order to motivate workers to rise up violently against their oppressors, Marxists had to kill off any hope in a heavenly life beyond this one and any fear of divine punishment. They had to replace a God-man with a man-God. But human beings are fallen creatures, not man-Gods. For this reason, no New Socialist Man ever emerged.

Two decades ago, when communism still posed a worldwide threat, a Romanian pastor named Josif Ton wrote of the contradiction that lies at the heart of a Marxist view of humanity. "[They teach] their pupils that life is the product of chance combinations of matter, that it is governed by Darwinian laws of adaptation and survival, and that it is man's only chance. There is no afterlife, no 'savior' to reward self-sacrifice or to punish egoism or rapacity. After the pupils have been thus taught, I am sent in to teach them to be noble and honorable men and women, expending all their energies on doing good for the benefit of society, even to the point of self-sacrifice. They must be courteous, tell only the truth, and live a morally pure life. But they lack motivation for goodness. They see that in a purely material world only he who hurries and grabs for himself possesses anything. Why should they be self-denying and honest? What motive can be offered them to live lives of usefulness to others?"

The *Pravda* editors conceded to us that they did not know how to motivate people to show compassion. A recent campaign to raise funds for the children of Chernobyl had foundered. The average Soviet citizen would rather spend his money on drink than support needy children. Their own polls had revealed that 70 percent of Soviet parents would not allow their children to have contact with a disabled child; 80 percent would not give money to help; some advocated infanticide. "How do you reform, change, motivate people?" the editors asked us. "How do you get people to be good?"

The editors' questions point to the second major flaw in Marxist anthropology. Early communists believed that they—not God—were the ones to determine morality, which could then be enforced from the top down. Seventy-four years of communism proved beyond all doubt that goodness cannot be legislated from the Kremlin and enforced at the point of a gun. In a great irony, attempts to compel morality tend to produce rebellious subjects and tyrannical rulers.

Worse, the communist rulers who made decisions about morality tragically recapitulated the first flaw: they too were fallen creatures. Moral principles shifted depending on who was in power. *Pravda* was now showing admirable compassion by raising funds for the victims of the Chernobyl disaster. But the same newspaper had, for example, shown no compassion whatever for the children victims of Stalin's enforced starvation of the Ukraine. What "higher law" determined when compassion applied and when it did not? *Pravda* had no answer.

I came away from Russia with the strong sense that we Christians would do well to relearn basic lessons of theology. Some of my friends seem almost embarrassed by doctrines like the Fall and original sin. "Christianity has such a pessimistic view of human nature," they say.

Others wish that God would play a more heavy-handed role in human affairs. "He allows too much freedom," they say. "Why doesn't God interfere more? Why does he let so much evil go unpunished in this life?"

In Russia, I saw the tragic results of the alternatives—an optimistic view of human nature and a morality based on compulsion, not inner transformation. It was a darkly sobering reminder of what happens when human beings ignore God's revelation and come up with their own.

Chapter 30

# The Wall Comes
# Tumbling Down

The reason formerly communist countries so quickly opened their doors to Christians after the collapse of Marxism traces back to the testimony of Christians who stayed faithful to their calling. They, too, are part of the untold story.

In East Germany, one of the few Eastern European countries with a Protestant majority, for forty years the church sought ways to serve the "city of God" while living in an officially atheistic "city of the world." Since many avenues (such as television and radio) were closed, early on the church adopted a commitment to care for the neediest members of society, especially the profoundly disabled. And they met together regularly for worship and prayer.

Although Jesus spoke of a "kingdom that is within you," throughout history the church has faced a constant temptation to form alliances with external centers of power. The U.S. church faces just that temptation today, with its emphasis on politics rather than spirituality. In a nation like East Germany under communism, that possibility did not exist. Christians there had no "power base" as such, none but the power of love and prayer.

Yet, against all odds, when the decisive moment for change finally arrived in the Eastern Bloc, the church led the way in a peaceful revolution. East Germans look back on October 9, 1989, as *die Wende,* the "turning point." The crucial event took place, appropriately enough, in Leipzig, a bastion of the Reformation where Luther preached in the sixteenth century and Bach played the organ in the eighteenth.

During 1989, four churches in Leipzig (including Bach's Thomaskirche) were holding weekly prayer meetings every Monday evening at five. The prayer meetings had begun seven years before, in 1982, when Pastor Christian Fuehrer invited his parishioners to gather to pray for peace. The pastors conducted the old Lutheran hymns, addressed their congregations with the Bible in one hand and the daily newspaper in the other, and led rounds of prayer. In this way they tried to give meaning and hope to the beleaguered East Germans. At first a handful of Christians, a few dozen at most, assembled.

Gradually, though, the congregations for these prayer meetings began to swell, attracting not just faithful Christians but also political dissidents and ordinary citizens. The church was the one place where the communist state allowed freedom of assembly. After each meeting, the groups would join together and walk through the dark streets of the old city, holding candles and banners—a most benign form of political protest. Virtually every protest demonstration in the entire country began in this way, with worship.

Eventually, news media from the West picked up the story. Alarmed, the communist hierarchy debated how to stamp out the peaceful marches. Secret police surrounded the churches, sometimes roughing up the marchers. But the crowds in Leipzig kept growing: hundreds, thousands, then fifty thousand.

Pastor Wonneberger of the St. Nikolai Church found himself in an unexpected role as de facto leader of the movement. He preached peace and gave practical advice on techniques of non-violence even as the secret police phoned in death threats and posted lookouts around his church.

On October 9, nearly everyone expected the political pressure to reach a critical mass. East Berlin was celebrating the forty-year anniversary of the communist state and viewed the marches in Leipzig as a provocation. Police and army units moved into Leipzig in force, and East German leader Erich Honecker gave them instructions to shoot the demonstrators. The country braced for a replay of Tiananmen Square. Leipzig's Lutheran bishop warned of a massacre, hospitals cleared emergency rooms, and churches and concert halls agreed to open their doors in case demonstrators needed quick refuge.

When time came for a prayer meeting at Nikolai Church, two thousand Communist Party members rushed inside to occupy all the seats. The church simply opened its seldom-used balconies, and a thousand protesters also crowded inside. The *Christian Century* reports that the service itself was a turning point: party members who attended with the intention of disrupting things realized for the first time that the church was indeed working for peaceful change.

No one knows for sure why the military held their fire that night. Egon Krenz, the short-lived successor to Honecker, took personal credit for rescinding the order. Some theorize that Mikhail Gorbachev himself telephoned a warning to Honecker. Others believe the army was simply cowed by the huge crowds. But everyone credits the prayer vigils in Leipzig for kindling the process of momentous change. In the end, 70,000 people marched peacefully through downtown Leipzig. The following Monday, 120,000 marched. A week later, 500,000 turned out— nearly the entire population of Leipzig.

In early November the largest march of all took place, almost 1 million people marching peacefully through East Berlin. Erich Honecker resigned, humiliated. Police refused to fire on the demonstrators. At midnight on November 9, something no one had even dared pray for happened: a gap opened up in the hated Berlin Wall. East Germans streamed through the checkpoints, past guards who had always obeyed orders to "shoot to kill." Not a single life was lost as throngs of people marching with candles brought down a government.

Like a windstorm of pure air driving out pollution, the peaceful revolution spread across the globe. In 1989 alone, ten nations comprising more than half a billion people—Poland, East Germany, Hungary, Czechoslovakia, Bulgaria, Romania, Albania, Yugoslavia, Mongolia, the Soviet Union—experienced nonviolent revolutions.

As Bud Bultman, a producer and writer for CNN, wrote: "We in the media watched in astonishment as the walls of totalitarianism came crashing down. But in the rush to cover the cataclysmic events, the story behind the story was overlooked. We trained our cameras on hundreds of thousands of people praying for freedom, votive candles in hand, and yet we missed the transcendent dimension, the explicitly spiritual and religious character of the story. We looked right at it and could not see it."

Some did see it. East Germans still speak of those days as a miracle. "Whether or not prayers really move mountains, they certainly mobilized the population of Leipzig," reported the *New Republic*. "To hear them sing 'A Mighty Fortress Is Our God' is enough to make you believe it." Several weeks after the October 9 turning point, a huge banner appeared across a Leipzig street: *Wir danken Dir, Kirche* (WE THANK YOU, CHURCH).

Chapter 31

# Big Nanny Is Watching

Polish playwright Janusz Glowacki recalls visiting a "This Is America" exhibit in Warsaw during the darkest days of Stalinism. While listening to a decadent boogie-woogie sound track, he gravely filed past displays of loud ties, gaudy billboards, KKK crosses, and even insects from Colorado that were supposedly dropped from planes at night to devour socialists' potatoes.

"The exhibition was meant to evoke horror, disgust, and hatred," Glowacki writes. "It had, however, the opposite effect. Thousands of Varsovians, dressed in their holiday best, waited every day in lines as long as those to see Lenin's Tomb and in solemn silence looked at the display, listened respectfully to the boogie-woogie, wanting in this way, at least, to manifest their blind and hopeless love for the United States."

Now, more than a decade after the astonishing changes in Europe, Poles and even Russians can freely design their own loud ties and gaudy billboards and compose their own boogie-woogie.

Against all odds, Western culture triumphed, with very few shots being fired. The Cold War ended; the Red Threat vanished. Now what?

Author Neil Postman *(Amusing Ourselves to Death)* suggests that though we seem to have escaped George Orwell's *1984*, we are still in dire peril from Huxley's *Brave New World*. People often confuse those two books, but they present quite different visions of the future. Maybe it's not Big Brother we should fear, but Big Nanny.

Orwell warned against an external enemy that relies on violence and propaganda to impose its will—something like communism or Nazism, both of which Orwell knew well. In contrast, Huxley warned against a more subtle enemy from within. People will gladly trade away their freedom and autonomy for a technology that promises comfort, safety, and amusement, he predicted. Orwell's villains used a pain machine to enforce their decrees; Huxley's villains relied on pleasure. Orwell's regime banned books; in Huxley's fantasy, books are plentiful but no one wants to read them.

Since 1984 has come and gone, with its threat fast receding, perhaps it is time to update Huxley's gentle nightmare. What would a "Brave New Society" look like?

1. A Brave New Society *repairs the defects in human personality*. Neurophysiologist José M. R. Delgado made a splash a few years back when he brought a charging bull to a dead stop by pressing the small button of a radio transmitter. (He had implanted an electrode in the bull's brain.) The title of his book describing this and other experiments says it well: *Physical Control of the Mind: Toward a Psychocivilized Society*.

   Open the spigot of government funds, say the

behavioral scientists, and we will identify the physiological bases of violence, addictions, and sexual and personality disorders. Then we can repair them through drugs or surgery.

Admittedly, a defect-free society may forfeit some valuable contributions from deviants. Would Beethoven, Schubert, and Brahms have created such music if their personality disorders had been repaired? We may have lost Jerome's Vulgate translation of the Bible, which served the church for one thousand years (he worked on it as a means of sublimating sexual desire), and Augustine may have watered down his *Confessions*. But just think how Abraham Lincoln—who rarely smiled, struggled with depression, and was married to a probable psychopath—might have been improved.

2. A Brave New Society *simplifies morality*. For centuries, church and state have hacked their way through a thicket of issues relating to sexuality and social justice. The new society dispenses with such notions as absolute truth and "inalienable rights." Only two principles matter: kindness and tolerance.

Politically correct thinking, based on kindness and tolerance, will insist on certain cultural adjustments. *Huckleberry Finn* and the Brothers Grimm will need a complete reworking. Anti-Semitic passages in Shakespeare must be excised. Can a Politically Correct Bible be far behind? (Zacchaeus was, after all, not "short," but "vertically challenged.")

3. A Brave New Society *solves problems through technology*. C. S. Lewis wrote, "For the wise men of old, the cardinal problem of human life was how to conform the soul to objective reality, and the solution was wisdom, self-discipline, and virtue. For the modern mind, the cardinal

problem is how to subdue reality to the wishes of man, and the solution is a technique."

We apply the criteria "developed, less-developed, underdeveloped," to Brave New Societies, avoiding such value-laden words as *just, moral, good.* Sad-eyed prophets like Solzhenitsyn used to argue that the suffering East could teach spiritual values to the materialistic West. I haven't heard that argument lately; the East is too busy trying to catch up to the economic standards of the West.

Africa and parts of Asia seem beyond our technological capacity to fix. They'll have their place in the Brave New Society, too: we'll watch two-minute reports on the devastation, sandwiched in between the sports and weather. Such an attitude has good precedent, dating back at least to Boccaccio's *Decameron.* During the Black Death, some young men and women took refuge in a well-protected castle. While carts gathered up the dead outside, these fortunate few devoted themselves to pleasure and games, telling the famous stories imagined by Boccaccio.

4. A Brave New Society *elevates entertainment above all other values.* To get a measure of how much we value entertainment, consider that a good baseball pitcher earns five times as much for an evening's work as a high school physics teacher earns in a year.

George Orwell feared a Big Brother whose projected image would intrude in every home. The screens are in place now, but we choose the images we want, and the bottom line is entertainment. As media scholar David Thorburn puts it, we can only stand in awe of "television's genius for marketing banality."

American families watch television five to seven hours a day, demonstrating an obsession with entertainment unmatched in history. Naturally, the medium affects the message. Watch *Sesame Street* for three minutes and you'll see what education looks like when forced through an entertainment grid. Or, compare the successful televangelist programs with the average local church service.

I am reminded of an old quote from Henry David Thoreau, who had a disturbingly stunted view: "Our inventions are wont to be pretty toys, which distract our attention from serious things. They are but improved means to an unimproved end, an end which it was already but too easy to arrive at. . . . We are in great haste to construct a magnetic telegraph from Maine to Texas; but Maine and Texas, it may be, have nothing important to communicate."

How close are we to achieving the Brave New Society? A recent visit to the British Museum Library gave me pause. One room displays original letters and manuscript pages from great authors, arranged chronologically. I spent several hours there, proceeding from Shakespeare and Donne to Elizabeth Barrett Browning and Jane Austen and Virginia Woolf. Finally I reached the most recent manuscript collection. There, displayed in a formal wooden case with gold leaf lettering, was the scrawled original of one of the most famous songs of the past century: "Oh yeah, oh yeah, I wanna hold your hand." The poet had captured the spirit of the age precisely. Daniel Boorstin, former librarian of Congress and director of the Smithsonian National Museum of American History, offers this assessment of contemporary culture:

When we pick up our newspaper at breakfast, we expect— we even demand—that it bring us momentous events since the night before. We turn on the car radio as we drive to work and expect "news" to have occurred since the

morning newspaper went to press. Returning in the
evening, we expect our house not only to shelter us, to
keep us warm in winter and cool in summer, but to relax
us, to dignify us, to encompass us with soft music and
interesting hobbies, to be a playground, a theatre, and a bar.
We expect our two-week vacation to be romantic, exotic,
cheap and effortless. We expect a far-away atmosphere if we
go to a near-by place; and we expect everything to be
relaxing, sanitary, and Americanized if we go to a far-away
place. We expect new heroes every season, a literary
masterpiece every month, a dramatic spectacular every
week, a rare sensation every night. We expect everybody to
feel free to disagree, yet we expect everybody to be loyal,
not to rock the boat or take the Fifth Amendment. We
expect everybody to believe deeply in his religion, yet not
to think less of others for not believing. We expect our
nation to be strong and great and vast and varied and
prepared for every challenge; yet we expect our "national
purpose" to be clear and simple, something that gives
direction to the lives of two hundred million people and yet
can be bought in a paperback at the corner drugstore for a
dollar.

We expect anything and everything. We expect the
contradictory and the impossible. We expect compact cars
which are spacious; luxurious cars which are economical.
We expect to be rich and charitable, powerful and merciful,
active and reflective, kind and competitive. We expect to be
inspired by mediocre appeals for "excellence," to be made
literate by illiterate appeals for literacy. We expect to eat and
stay thin, to be constantly on the move and ever more
neighbourly, to go to the "church of our choice" and yet
feel its guiding power over us, to revere God and to be
God.

Never have people been more the masters of their

environment. Yet never has a people felt more deceived and disappointed.

Ah, Brave New World! Boorstin neglected to mention that the word *culture,* as in "modern culture," also refers to something grown in an artificial medium. For instance, a virus.

# Chapter 32

# Tremors Underground

In 1983 an American businessman landed at the Beijing Airport, was met on the tarmac by a limousine, and traveled to a meeting downtown without seeing a single other vehicle. His driver concentrated instead on dodging some of the city's 8 million bicycles. A mere twenty years later, in 2003, the Chinese government announced that the 2 millionth car had been registered in Beijing.

China is well on target to make the twenty-first century a "China century." Thirty-five percent of the world's ocean freighters are delivering goods and raw materials to feed China's superheated economy. Heavy equipment companies estimate that 40 percent of the world's construction cranes are now operating there. In Beijing alone, two thousand high-rise buildings are under construction (though the government has decreed that all cranes must be gone by 2007 so as not to spoil the backdrop of the 2008 Olympics, China's showcase to the world).

Meanwhile, under the radar screen of the world's press, the Chinese church has been growing at an even faster rate than the economy. In 1950 the communist government expelled seven thousand missionaries and did its best to control Christianity through registered "Three-Self" churches (government-regulated churches dedicated to self-administration, self-support, and self-propagation). For twenty years this strategy appeared to be working, until in the 1970s an underground house church movement sprang up as if by spontaneous generation.

Even the Chinese government admits that Protestant Christians have increased from 1 million in 1950 to 16 million today. But these figures do not account for the many millions who meet secretly in home congregations. David Aikman, former Beijing bureau chief for *Time* magazine, suggests in his book *Jesus in Beijing* that Christians may number as many as 80 million—this in an officially atheist state that has relentlessly persecuted believers.

Aikman was so intrigued by rumors coming out of China that he moved to Hong Kong to research the phenomenon. It is plausible, says Aikman, "that 20–30% of China's population will be Christians in thirty years' time." Inevitably, Christians will find their way into key positions of leadership. "China will be Christianized if the current trend continues," Aikman concludes.


I interviewed four representatives of the Chinese house church movement on a trip to Beijing in 2004. My hosts had rented two hotel rooms and we moved back and forth between the rooms for each interview (so that, if arrested, each of the Chinese Christians could not implicate the others). Although the rooms were stuffy and smelled like insecticide, we dared not open windows lest representatives of the Public Security Bureau lurked outside.

I had brought along signed copies of some of my books in Chinese, but my hosts requested that I tear out the page with my signature. An original signature on a book would prove that church leaders had had direct contact with the West, which would further jeopardize their safety. Clearly, I had a lot to learn about operating in an environment hostile to religion.

I anticipated most eagerly our scheduled meeting with Pastor Allen Yuan, a patriarch of the house church movement who has courageously defied government attempts to control his activities. Pastor Yuan survived twenty-two years of hard labor in prison, and on his release immediately resumed baptizing new converts. A visit to his home by Billy Graham in 1994 attracted world attention, and when President Clinton visited China in 1998, the government forbade any of the two thousand foreign journalists from seeing him.

Sadly, Pastor Yuan called the hotel to report that because the annual meeting of the Communist Party was taking place in Beijing, authorities had again forbidden him to meet with any foreigners.

Lao San, supervisor of some fifty house church leaders, traveled ten hours on a night train to tell his story. He began preaching at the age of twelve and devotes himself to the rural Christian community, comprising mostly uneducated farmers. He described the average church service, two to three hours long, which includes much singing and loud praying and a sermon that averages an hour in length. The churches move from home to home and keep to small, discreet groups. Lao San seemed afraid. Local authorities had recently been harassing him, and I sensed the very fact of meeting with a Westerner struck fear in his heart. He told me he keeps his precious Bible buried in a container in his back yard. Lao San kept his head down and answered my questions in terse, brief sentences.

Next came Brother Joshua, a stocky farmer with snow-white hair. A third-generation Christian, he can trace his faith lineage back to some of the old-time missionaries. Unlike Lao San, Joshua spoke proudly and volubly about all his activities. Joshua lost his job during the Cultural Revolution, spent six months in prison, and is now supported by Japanese Christians who use his services for Bible distribution. He stocks a large barn with Bibles brought in by Japanese "tourists," and over the years Joshua has distributed hundreds of thousands of these Bibles. (Although 25 million Bibles have been legally printed and sold since 1987, more than half of China's Christians don't have access to one.)

The most impressive visitor was Brother Shi, a bright and passionate forty-four-year-old who did not fit the profile of peasant Christianity. Indeed, as a teenager Shi headed up his province's Communist Youth League and later served as a Red Guard. He used to pass by a Three-Self church on his bicycle each day en route to party headquarters, and it puzzled him that whereas he had to work hard to attract young people to the party, the Three-Self church was always packed.

One day he decided to attend, and the vibrant testimonies of Christians puzzled him further. He bought a Bible and read it through, from Genesis to Revelation. A few months later he announced to the party chief that he was becoming a Christian. The chief jumped to his feet and shouted that he was making a serious mistake. He was cutting off all chance of advancement in life, throwing away a bright future. As Shi left the room, the chief called the boy's father to report this treachery.

Shi's father met him at the door with oaths. "You have done a very bad thing to us!" he said. "I fought against the Christian Chiang Kai-shek, and I fought against the Christians in Korea, and now I have Jesus in my own house!" He kicked Shi out of the house, throwing his belongings in the dirt outside. For several days Shi slept in a friend's office. He would see his father on the street and try to speak, but his father always turned his head.

A decade later, after the miraculous healing of his grandson, Shi's father at last began to melt. Today he, too, is a Christian.

Brother Shi must travel constantly, eluding police through narrow escapes. "I've never been arrested, thanks to the help of churches who hide me," he says. "Once I got away just three minutes before the police came." The house churches, recognizing Shi's leadership skills, have promoted him so that he now supervises 260,000 Christians in his province. He sees his wife, also a renowned church leader, only once a year.

Just as our meetings concluded, someone knocked on the door. It was Pastor Yuan, a sprightly senior citizen who had decided to defy the ban and meet with a foreigner anyway. "I'm ninety years old and I've spent twenty-two years in prison—what are they going to do to me?" he said with a grin. He gave me a photo of the 453 Chinese believers he baptized in 2003.

Before going to China, I met with one of the missionaries who had been expelled in 1950. "We felt so sorry for the church we left behind," he said. "They had no one to teach them, no printing presses, no seminaries, no one to run their clinics and orphanages. No resources, really, except the Holy Spirit." It appears the Holy Spirit did just fine.

# Chapter 33

# Cry, the Beloved Continent

Two months before visiting China, I made a journey to the beautiful land of South Africa. While China cautiously emerges from strict totalitarian rule, South Africa is celebrating its second decade of freedom from a strict apartheid government.

The church reveals a similar contrast. Whereas the church in China operates mostly out of sight, Christians in South Africa operate boisterously and in the open. Desmond Tutu, an Anglican bishop, won the Nobel Peace Prize during the fight against apartheid and remains a national hero. Some 70 percent of South Africans attend church, one of the highest percentages in the world. Even so, a terrifying specter of disease looms over both nation and church, clouding the future of both.

But who wants to hear about AIDS in Africa? Relief agencies such as World Vision and World Concern face that question while trying to raise funds to fight this world health catastrophe. Americans, overwhelmed by the magnitude of problems in Africa, wonder if anything can help. Though they may not say so directly, many American Christians also can't help thinking "They deserve it." After all, doesn't AIDS in Africa spread mainly through sexual promiscuity?

Indeed, the visitor to Africa finds a different sexual landscape. Adolescent boys celebrate their rite of passage into adulthood with a public circumcision ceremony; in major cities you can see plastic "circumcision tents" near airports, inside expressway cloverleafs, or wherever open land remains. Later, the new "men" may celebrate their adult status with sexual exploits. The continent has a long history of polygamy, and in places like South Africa, the practice of separating male workers from their families further broke down marital ties.

No one is exempt: in confidential surveys by World Vision, 72 percent of South African pastors admit to having had extramarital affairs, with an average of three to four partners each. Muslims proudly point out that in Africa, the great frontier between Islam and Christianity, Islam is gaining momentum, in large part because the Christians in sub-Saharan Africa are dying at a faster rate, while strict Sharia law keeps down promiscuity, and hence the HIV rate, in Muslim areas.

Yet a finger-wagging approach does little to help the problem. Bruce Wilkinson stirred up a hornet's nest when he lectured African church leaders about the sinful aspects of the AIDS epidemic. In Uganda, some evangelical churches require mandatory HIV testing and will not marry a couple unless both test negative for the virus—thus driving young couples away from the church.

Nor does denial help. In South Africa, which has the world's largest number of people living with HIV/AIDS, President Thabo Mbeki has openly questioned the link between AIDS and the HIV virus. Recently he declared that he personally knew of no one who had died of AIDS. That may be technically true (AIDS lowers the body's resistance to other diseases, which do the killing), but his attitude has set back the work of AIDS educators who are trying to alert Africans to the urgency of the crisis.

By any measure, AIDS workers face a herculean task. In parts of Africa, life expectancy has sunk from sixty-five to thirty-three, a level not seen since the nineteenth century. I heard many statistics about AIDS in South Africa, and none more stunning than this: researchers predict that in some areas, half the youngsters under fifteen will die within ten years. Imagine a teacher walking into a classroom and looking at the eager young faces, knowing that half will soon be dead.

World Vision workers in southern Africa told me that self-stigma is their biggest obstacle, which keeps infected people from getting tested or seeking treatment. When Botswana (with a 38 percent HIV infection rate, the world's highest) offered free medication for those with AIDS, only 1 percent of the population responded, due to the stigma.

An HIV-infected worker who got the virus through a blood transfusion told me, "To those who lack compassion for Africans because 'they deserve it,' I remind them that half the infections come about when a promiscuous partner infects someone 'innocent' and unsuspecting." All too often, HIV gets passed on to the resulting child as well, or else that child may become one of the millions of AIDS orphans who are now growing up in Africa.

I visited a Christian care facility in Johannesburg for those in the advanced stages of the disease, and saw children with matchstick arms and vacant eyes who lie in beds all day awaiting the next seizure. Volunteer "mothers" visit to hold and rock them. New advances in treatment offer hope for some children, but meanwhile many are dying. One nearby community used to average two funerals per week; it now has seventy-five. A Christian center in Cape Town that teaches young people printing skills used to specialize in wedding invitations; it now supports itself by selling funeral programs.

Of all countries on the continent, South Africa is the one

where you will most likely hear the words *hope* and *transformation*. Larger-than-life heroes such as Desmond Tutu and Nelson Mandela still inspire the nation with the power of grace and reconciliation. AIDS presents a wholly different crisis from the one posed by an entrenched apartheid government. That was a crisis of theology and of justice. This is a crisis of compassion, requiring not a change in laws and government, but of hearts.

We can look at the children with stolen futures, at an entire continent whose future hangs in the balance, and ask questions of God. Or we can look at the same problems and realize that these are God's questions to us. Who cares about AIDS in Africa?

# Chapter 34

# Doubting the Doomsayers

In 2004, I worked on a tribute-edition update of the book *Fear-fully and Wonderfully Made*, which I had coauthored with Dr. Paul Brand in 1980. (He died in 2003.) During that process, I reviewed a passage spelling out the huge gap between developed countries and the developing world. I had just received an e-mail indicating that little has changed since 1980. The anonymous author reported that 80 percent of the world's people still live in substandard housing, 70 percent are unable to read, and 50 percent suffer from malnutrition.

My curiosity piqued, I spent several days tracking down statistics from the UN, Habitat for Humanity, and other authoritative sources, only to find that the anonymous e-mail is downright wrong. In fact, the world has made major strides in the last few decades.

Thirty years ago the global rate of illiteracy was 47 percent;

now only 20 percent of adults cannot read. The percentage of people suffering from malnutrition has dropped by more than half, as has the percentage of people living in substandard housing. Three of four people used to have no access to clean water; now three of four people have such access. One billion people got clean drinking water in the 1980s alone.

Perhaps the most significant change has occurred in population growth. In 1968, Paul Ehrlich predicted in *The Population Bomb* that huge famines would occur in the 1970s and 1980s, with hundreds of millions of people starving to death. Nothing can prevent them, he declared. Those famines simply did not happen.

Population experts once forecast that world population would hit a high of 20 billion, causing an intolerable strain on earth's resources. That prediction was lowered to 15 billion, then 11 billion (the UN estimate in 1990), then 9 billion. Now some experts predict that the world's population will hit that lowered peak around 2050, and then maybe even decline.

The birthrate has fallen so dramatically that in Western Europe, Russia, and Japan, experts are now warning of the dire consequences of an aging population unreplenished by younger generations. Worldwide, the average woman used to bear six children; now she bears three. As developing countries improve economically, the birthrate drops.

Thirty years ago, one in eight children died in the first year of life; now half that proportion dies. (Just over a century ago, four in five children died of disease before they reached the age of five.) AIDS currently presents a major health challenge, especially in Africa, and yet we dare not minimize health triumphs: smallpox, a disease that in the nineteenth century killed *500 million* people, has been eradicated. The feared disease polio has nearly disappeared, and leprosy has seen large declines.

A huge economic gap remains between the developed world

and developing countries. Half the world's citizens still get by on less than two dollars a day. Even so, the World Bank estimates that the percentage of those living in absolute poverty has been cut almost in half, and per capita income has risen 60 percent. Ten million entrepreneurs have improved their lives through micro-enterprise loans.

According to the UN, overall conditions in the developing world improved more in the second half of the twentieth century than in the previous five hundred years. Although repressive regimes and brutal dictators dominate the news, according to Freedom House seventy-one more nations have become "free" or "partly free" in recent years.

Politicians and preachers decry the state of sexual morality in the United States. But the Centers for Disease Control and Prevention reports that the teenage birthrate has declined by 30 percent in the last decade while our abortion rate declined by almost half. Many surveys show that on sexual issues, teenagers are more conservative than their parents.

Such good news rarely captures the attention of the media, which continues to portray the world as teetering on the brink of cataclysm. Nor does it get much play from relief and development agencies, which have learned that donors respond best to crisis appeals.

As a journalist who often travels internationally, I am well aware of the major problems that face our planet: global warming, income disparity, terrorism and wars, SARS, AIDS, and other diseases. At the same time, I find it genuinely heartwarming to learn of the progress that has occurred during my lifetime.

A century ago, theological liberals rightly complained that conservative Christians cared for souls but not bodies. Liberals led the way in social reform. Now, evangelical organizations such as World Vision, World Concern, and Opportunity International are among the most prominent and effective dispensers of "common grace" to a needy world.

After several days of research, I paused to give thanks for this remarkable progress. I have learned to not believe everything I read on the Internet, and not believe everything I hear from doomsayers.

Part Six

✠

Finding

God

in

the

Cracks

Chapter 35

# Five Polluted Words

One day my wife, Janet, who was directing a senior citizens' program in one of Chicago's poorest neighborhoods, came across this quote: "The poor express their gratitude not by saying thanks but by asking for more." She had just spent an exhausting day and felt besieged by whiny, insistent demands for ever more help. That quote proved strangely comforting, she told me.

Why is it that the poor express their gratitude so indirectly? I wondered. Why don't they simply give thanks? After talking with Janet about her many experiences on the job, I concluded it is because of shame—shame over their need for help in the first place. I know how hard it is for me to ask someone else for help. What would it be like to live in a constant state of neediness?

More to the point, how can those of us who give to others do so without somehow undermining their sense of dignity? Due to my writer's instinct, I immediately started thinking of individual words, and I began to make a list. All of these words began as a pure expression of *giving* but became polluted over time. Such words litter the English language; taken together, they offer a strong warning about the dangers inherent in giving and receiving.

**P**ity. Deriving from the same root as "piety" and "pious," this word once denoted a high form of sacrificial love. God, a perfect Being without needs, nevertheless chose to give of himself to his creatures. God had pity on needy people, such as the Israelite slaves in Egypt. God's ultimate act of self-giving, the Incarnation, can actually be seen as an act of pity, motivated out of God's love for us fallen human creatures. On earth, Jesus often felt moved with compassion, or pity. Those who mimicked him—the rich having pity on the poor, for example—thus expressed God-like qualities.

That was the older meaning of the word, at least. Eventually emphasis shifted from the givers of pity to the recipients, who were seen as being weak and inferior. Now we hear the taunt, "I don't want your pity!" One who shows pity is condescending, even *un*loving—the meaning of the word has nearly inverted.

**Charity.** The IRS still recognizes the inherent goodness of this word—the agency grants tax exemptions for donations to "charitable" organizations—but surely it too has lost some luster. In the King James Version of 1611, chapter 13 of 1 Corinthians renders *charity* as a direct translation of *agape,* the most exalted form of love, the kind of love that most nearly resembles God's love. Charity flows from a person who is patient, kind, forgiving, humble; charity never fails to discern the best in people.

Yet once again the meaning became inverted over time: now no one wants to be a "charity case." We accept charity only in desperation, as a last resort.

**Condescend.** I view the entire Bible as a step-by-step history of God's con-descensions. To Adam in the garden, to Moses in the burning bush, to the Israelites in the glory cloud, and finally to all of us in the Incarnation, he con-descended, or "descended to be with" us. A true Christian follows that example, as the apostle Paul clearly outlined in this passage: "Your attitude should be the same as that of Christ Jesus: Who, being in the very nature God, did not consider equality with God something to be grasped, but made himself nothing, taking the very nature of a servant, being made in human likeness" (Philippians 2:5–7).

Once again, though, over time the word's meaning leached away. We have lost the fine art of condescension. Who of us would welcome the remark, "You're so condescending!"?

**Patronize.** I have a special fondness for this word, for artists, musicians, and, yes, writers were once relieved of everyday anxieties about earning a living due to the generosity of *patrons*. Nowadays, however, there are few patrons, and fewer still who would want to be called patronizing. The modern *Random House Dictionary* defines *patronize* as "To behave in an offensively *condescending* manner toward"!

**Paternalism.** Another fine word, badly tainted. The root comes from *pater*, or "father." In older days, a paternalistic person reminded others of a kindly father who cared for the needs of his children; now the image more resembles an insensitive stepfather who reeks of superiority as he stoops down to help his charges.

Why have these words changed in meaning? Each of them, once honorable and majestic, gradually melted like a wax statue into a sad lump barely resembling its former self. The words have changed, quite simply, because we humans have failed so often and so badly at the difficult task of giving. Perhaps an ancient Chinese proverb expresses the problem best: "Nothing atones for the insult of a gift but the love of the giver."

A Christian organization carrying out relief work in a needy country, my wife as she ministers one-on-one to senior citizens or the homeless, I as I confront a beggar on the street—each of us confronts the vast and perilous gap between the giver and the receiver. Government programs established with the highest of motives often founder for reasons that can be glimpsed in these polluted words. An institution cannot love; only people can love. As the proverb says, apart from love, giving becomes an insult.

We could all avoid these problems if we simply ignored the needy and associated with self-sufficient people exclusively. However, reaching out to the needy is not an option for the Christian. It is a command. As I have mentioned, I wrote a book entitled *Where Is God When It Hurts?* The real answer to that question, I learned, is another question: where is the church when it hurts? We followers of Jesus are God's primary response to the massive needs of the world. We are literally Christ's Body.

When Jesus lived here in a physical body, he spent time among the poor, the widowed, the paralyzed, and even those with dreaded diseases. People with leprosy, for example—the AIDS patients of ancient times—were required to cry out "Unclean! Unclean!" if anyone approached; touching such a person went against the laws of Moses. Yet Jesus defied law and custom by going up to leprosy patients and touching them—an act of astonishing condescension. That has been God's consistent pattern in all of history.

We in the church, God's Body on earth, are likewise called to move toward those who suffer. We are, after all, God's means of expressing his love to the world, which is why words such as *pity* and *charity* originated as religious words.

Can we reclaim these polluted words—or, if not the words, then at least the meaning behind them? I take some hope in the fact that all the words in the above list retain at least a glimmer of their theological origin. There is a way to make pity God-like; charity can convey a high form of love; condescension may lead to unity, not division; a patron may exalt, not demean, his subjects; paternalism may, in fact, remind us of our true state as children of a heavenly Father.

Indeed, I know of only one way to eliminate the great gap between giver and receiver, and that is a humble recognition that all of us are needy beggars, sustained each moment by the mercy of a sovereign God. Only as we experience God's grace as pure grace, not something we earned or worked for, can we offer love with no strings attached to another person in need. There is but one true Giver in the universe; all else are debtors.

# Chapter 36

# Healing While Rome Burns

On assignment for a charitable organization, I visited Myanmar, the former Burma, one of the most tightly controlled nations on earth. Local writers told me the capital city has one bookstore, to their knowledge the only bookstore for a population of 50 million. They joked that Myanmar has no copyright, but "copy left": they rely on foreigners who leave copies behind as their main source of books.

Billboards around town proclaimed the PEOPLE'S DESIRES in Stalinesque prose, such as REPORT ALL STOOGES TO THE AUTHORITIES. A taxi driver pointed to one such billboard and said to me, "Not people's desire—generals' desire." A troika runs the country with an iron fist, squeezing life out of the economy, stifling religion and the arts, and crushing any moves toward democracy.

Aung San Suu Kyi, who received the Nobel Peace Prize in 1991, has done her best to expose and oppose the brutality of

Myanmar's rulers. Daughter of a national hero, she lives under house arrest in Yangon (formerly Rangoon). Whenever she tries to leave, army vehicles blockade her car, creating incidents that attract the international press.

I met with representatives of a Christian relief organization that helps victims of AIDS there. By their estimate, fifty thousand AIDS orphans roam the streets of Myanmar, though the government officially denies any problem. Recently, relief workers visited Aung San Suu Kyi, a bold act that risked retaliation.

"Why are you helping these children?" asked the woman reverentially called "The Lady" by most Burmese. Aid to the needy helps prop up a corrupt regime, she said. They should let conditions grow so intolerable that citizens would rise up in revolt or the regime would simply collapse.

The relief organization agreed that her argument has a certain logic. Many South Africans supported international sanctions, which harmed people in the short term, in hopes that they might eventually help liberate them. In Miami, Cuban refugees use the same reasoning to oppose economic aid to Castro's beleaguered island.

In the end, though, the Christian relief workers could not simply close their eyes and sacrifice fifty thousand orphans to some political end. Through orphanages, clinics, and adoptive families, they are meeting human needs one at a time, as Christians through the ages have traditionally done.

Hearing my friends describe the dilemma in Myanmar got me thinking of problems in a wider context, encompassing the entire planet. Christians see our world as transitory, infected with evil, and destined for destruction. In words from 2 Peter, "The day of the Lord will come like a thief. The heavens will disappear with a roar; the elements will be destroyed by fire, and the earth and everything in it will be laid bare."

How should we live in view of such a future? The next verses address that very question: "Since everything will be destroyed in this way, what kind of people ought you to be?" The author urges his readers to "live holy and godly lives," to prepare for apocalypse by being spotless, blameless, and at peace with God.

Old Testament prophets and New Testament epistles give us glimpses of the future. Yet they admonish us to focus on behavior in the present, trusting God with the Big Picture. Some Christians I know tend to confuse those two perspectives. They shrug off destruction of the world's forests and pollution of its air and water—Won't the whole planet be destroyed, as Peter prophesied? In Middle East conflicts they always side with Israel, ignoring injustices against the Palestinians—Hasn't God promised to bless the chosen people in the latter days?

Such policies confuse our roles with God's. The prophets also predicted the Crucifixion, but that does not mean followers of Jesus should have helped nail him to the cross. The New Testament speaks of an Antichrist, but I will not knowingly vote for him even though doing so might hasten the second coming. Though I have some hints about the future, I must live in the present, treating the earth and its people with the same love and care that God invested in them at creation, acting out my faith that God will someday restore it to that graced state.

We take our brightest clue from Jesus, who knew better than anyone the ultimate fate of this planet and described it in terrifying detail. Nonetheless, he spent his time on earth healing the sick, raising the dead, helping widows and orphans, comforting prisoners, ministering to the poor. "Thy will be done on earth as it is in heaven," Jesus taught us to pray, and then proceeded to demonstrate exactly what that might look like. He showed little concern over the impact his acts of compassion might have on the longevity of the Roman Empire.

# Chapter 37

# Miracle on LaSalle Street

I first met Bill Leslie in a grungy pizza parlor after a DePaul University basketball game. I was surprised to find an overweight white man who dressed carelessly, talked too loud, and laughed uproariously at his own jokes. This was the minister of Chicago's renowned LaSalle Street Church?

Out of curiosity I attended LaSalle the following Sunday, and ended up staying there for thirteen years. I got to know Bill well, especially after my wife accepted a job directing one of the church's outreach programs. Bill talked too loud in the pulpit, too, and laughed at his own oft-repeated jokes, and occasionally slaughtered the English language. But he became our pastor, and we grew to love him, and when he died unexpectedly of a heart attack at the age of sixty, Janet and I joined many other Chicagoans in grieving the loss.

Bill Leslie served the same church for twenty-eight years, and what a time it was. The congregation met in a building whose walls can tell the history of Chicago: German-speaking Lutherans laid the cornerstone in 1882, and Italians, Japanese, and Appalachian whites all took turns in the building until hippies and then yuppies moved in. When Bill became pastor in 1961, the church stood midway between the richest and poorest communities of Chicago. Two blocks to the east lay the Gold Coast, average income over $50,000; two blocks to the west lay the Cabrini-Green housing project, average income under $3,000. While studying the biblical prophets' words on justice, LaSalle caught a vision of being a "bridge church" between the two neighborhoods.

After several years of commuting from the comfortable suburb of Wheaton, Bill Leslie heard God's call to join the neighborhood. It was 1968, the worst time possible for such a move. After Martin Luther King Jr.'s assassination, angry residents burned down thirty square blocks of buildings; the church stood intact amid the rubble, preserved because of its good reputation in the community. National Guardsmen patrolled the streets. The Leslies could find no one willing to insure their urban home.

A few years later, three men attacked Bill in the sanctuary, hoping to steal the morning offering. They hit him on the head with a bowling pin, stomped on his groin, and battered him with a fire extinguisher. Stripped of clothing, gagged, hog-tied, Bill lay in the vestibule and reconsidered his call to the city.

But he did not give up. Too much was happening in the fledgling congregation for him to walk away. Neighborhood outreach started when Sunday school teachers, noticing that many students could not read, offered tutoring classes after the Sunday service. The need was enormous—the local high school had a dropout rate of 75 percent. Soon busloads of students from nearby Wheaton College were making their way to LaSalle Street to help with one-on-one tutoring.

Since unemployment among the working-age population of Cabrini averaged 86 percent, most kids from the projects hung out on street corners all day. During summer months, someone in the neighborhood is shot an average of once every other day. Bill and others at the church saw a need for recreational programs. They bought a pool table, set up a basketball court, and raised money for football equipment (the high school team, with only thirteen helmets, was scrimmaging with seven players lined up on offense and six on defense). Before long an urban Young Life program had sprung up, affiliated with the church.

More needs surfaced. When a government study reported that a third of all dog and cat food was bought by senior citizens too poor to afford "people food," the church began a ministry to local seniors. To counter neighborhood abuse by the police and by landlords, an attorney quit his firm to begin a legal aid clinic, offering free legal representation to any Cabrini-Green resident with qualifying income. A counseling center was established, with sliding fees based on income.

In Chicago, as in most cities, half of all babies are born to single mothers, and soon the church founded a ministry to assist them as well. Bill was most proud, however, of a housing project that he first dreamed of when the church's annual budget was $20,000. Somehow, with LaSalle leading the way to secure grants and loans, the $11 million development became a reality. Economically and racially mixed, Atrium Village is credited with anchoring the community and reversing neighborhood decay.

Bill Leslie was a most unlikely pioneer. He was disheveled, disorganized (several times I waited in vain for Bill, who had forgotten our appointment or gone to the wrong restaurant), and hardly a promising candidate for racial reconciliation (he had been student body president at the strictly segregated Bob Jones University). Yet he, as much as anyone, was responsible for pointing the evangelical church back to the city and for reminding us that Jesus came to redeem communities as well as individual souls. He helped found a program to train young seminarians in urban ministry. Now, in many U.S. cities, young Christians are moving in as pioneers to lead the way in community development.

Three decades in the inner city took a toll on Bill and his family. He never did learn to say no. At the memorial service, one woman glowingly recalled that Bill had spent eight hours counseling her the day before he departed on a monthlong trip to Greece. A member of the congregation acknowledged the other side, addressing the Leslie family directly: "I'm sorry that Bill gave us so much and had so little left over for you."

Bill Leslie did some things wrong, but he got one thing right: he understood the grace of God. Grace became the church's theme: its fifty-year anniversary banquet featured a large banner that read THIS FAR BY GRACE.

Bill Leslie recognized his own endless need for grace, preached it almost every Sunday, and offered it to everyone around him in starkly practical ways. Because of his faithfulness, the Near North Side of Chicago is a very different place today. And so, I believe, is Heaven.

Yvonne Delk, a powerful African-American woman who leads the Community Renewal Society, summed up Bill's life with simple eloquence, "He was biblical without being fundamentalist, spiritual without being withdrawn from the world, and actively engaged with the world but not conformed to it. You have fought the good fight, Bill, you have finished the course, you have kept the faith. We are grateful for a man sent from God to Chicago whose name is Bill."

# Chapter 38

# The Surprise of Faith

The Gospels normally use the miracles to stress Jesus' power and authority. At least nine stories, however, focus on faith. "Your faith has healed you," Jesus would say, shifting attention from himself to the healed person. Miraculous power did not come from his side alone; somehow it depended on an individual's response.

I once read through all the miracle stories together and found they reveal remarkably different degrees of faith. A few people demonstrated bold, unshakable faith, such as a centurion who told Jesus he need not bother with a visit—just a word would heal his servant long-distance. "I tell you the truth, I have not found anyone in Israel with such great faith," Jesus remarked, astonished.

Another time, a foreign woman pursued Jesus as he was seeking peace and quiet. At first Jesus answered her not a word. Then he replied sharply, telling her he was sent to the lost sheep of Israel, not to "dogs"—referring to her status as a Gentile. But nothing could deter this Canaanite woman, and her perseverance won Jesus over. "Woman, you have great faith!" he said.

Jesus seemed impressed that, as foreigners, these were the least likely people to demonstrate great faith. Why should a centurion and a Canaanite, who had no Jewish roots, put their trust in a Messiah his own countrymen had trouble accepting?

These stories threaten me, because seldom do I have such outstanding faith. Unlike the Canaanite woman, I am easily discouraged by the silence of God. When my prayers are not soon answered, I am tempted to give up and not ask again. I identify more readily with the wavering man who declared to Jesus, "I believe, Lord. Help me overcome my unbelief!" All too often I find myself echoing those words, dangling somewhere between belief and unbelief, wondering how much I miss out on by my lack of faith.

Sometimes Jesus was amazed by the *lack* of faith he came across. Mark gives this extraordinary comment about Jesus' visit to his hometown: "He could not do any miracles there, except lay his hands on a few sick people and heal them." In a strange way, God's power was "paralyzed" by a lack of faith.

To my surprise, I noticed as I read through the stories that the people who knew Jesus best sometimes faltered in their faith. It was his own neighbors who doubted him. John the Baptist, who had proclaimed, "Look, the Lamb of God!" and heard a voice from Heaven at Jesus' baptism, later questioned him. And several times Jesus remarked with dismay on the twelve disciples' faithlessness.

Jesus' three most intimate disciples saw a dramatic miracle shortly before his death. On the Mount of Transfiguration, Jesus' face shone like the sun and his clothes became dazzling white. A cloud enveloped the disciples and inside that cloud, to their astonishment, they found two long-dead giants of Jewish history: Moses and Elijah. It was too much for the dazed disciples to take in; when God spoke audibly in the cloud, they fell down, terror-stricken. Yet what impact did such a stupendous event have? Shortly, the eyewitnesses of the Transfiguration joined the rest of the Twelve in abandoning—denying, in Peter's case—Jesus in his hour of deepest need.

We easily forget that Judas had for three years watched Jesus work great miracles and listened to his teaching; even so, he betrayed Jesus. Another disciple, "doubting Thomas," gained a reputation as a skeptic, but in truth all the disciples showed a lack of faith. None of them believed the wild reports the women brought back from the empty tomb. Even after Jesus appeared to them in person, says Matthew, "some doubted."

A curious law of reversal seems to be at work in the Gospels: faith appears where least expected and falters where it should be thriving.

I remember my first visit to Old Faithful in Yellowstone National Park. Rings of Japanese and German tourists surrounded the geyser, their video cameras trained like weapons on the famous hole in the ground. A large digital clock stood beside the spot, predicting twenty-four minutes until the next eruption.

My wife and I passed the countdown in the dining room of Old Faithful Inn overlooking the geyser. When the digital clock reached one minute, we along with every other diner left our seats and rushed to the windows to see the big wet event.

I noticed that immediately, as if on signal, a crew of busboys and waiters descended on the tables to refill water glasses and clear away dirty dishes. When the geyser went off, we tourists oohed and aahed and clicked our cameras; a few spontaneously applauded. But, glancing back over my shoulder, I saw that not a single waiter or busboy—not even those who had finished their chores—looked out the huge windows. Old Faithful, grown entirely too familiar, had lost its power to impress them.

Once, our church back in Chicago faced something of a crisis. The pastor had left, attendance was flagging, a community outreach program now seemed threatened. The leadership suggested an all-night vigil of prayer.

Several people raised questions. Was it safe, given our inner-city neighborhood? Should we hire guards or escorts for the parking lot? What if no one showed up? At length we discussed the logistics and the "practicality" of such an event. Nevertheless, the night of prayer was scheduled.

To my surprise the poorest members of the congregation, a group of senior citizens from a housing project, were the ones who responded most enthusiastically to the prayer vigil. I could not help wondering how many of their prayers had gone unanswered over the years—they lived in the projects, after all, amid crime, poverty, and suffering—yet still they showed a childlike trust in the power of prayer. "How long do you want to stay—an hour or two?" we asked, thinking of the logistics of van shuttles. "Oh, we'll stay all night," they replied.

One black woman in her nineties, who walks with a cane and can barely see, explained to a staff member why she wanted to spend the night sitting on the hard pews of a church in an unsafe neighborhood. "You see, they's lots of things we can't do in this church. We ain't so educated, and we ain't got as much energy as some of you younger folks. But we can pray. We got time, and we got faith. Some of us don't sleep much anyway. We can pray all night if needs be."

And so they did. Meanwhile, a bunch of yuppies in a downtown church learned anew a lesson of faith from the Gospels: faith appears where least expected and falters where it should be thriving.

# Chapter 39

# The Alchemy of Memory

One Christmas, I got into an extended conversation with my grandmother, who was born in 1898 and died in 2000, having just made it into her third century. "Who was your favorite president?" I asked. She thought for a moment and replied, "Roosevelt."

"I can understand that," I replied. "After all, he led us during World War II and started many important programs, like Social Security."

"Oh, no," she interrupted. "I mean Teddy Roosevelt. Now there was a real man!" She told me about going to see him at a whistle-stop tour in the 1912 election. She was already a teenager then.

Later, when I was discussing my visit to Russia to witness the fall of communism, my grandmother piped in, "Oh, yes, I remember when the communists first took over [in 1917]. That was scary. But I didn't think those boys would last." Being older than the century gives one a certain perspective: she had watched the full cycle as a powerful ideology appeared on the scene, burst into light, then faded away like a dying star.

As I probed my grandmother's astonishing memory, I noticed a trend that seems almost universal in the reminiscences of older people: they tend to recall difficult, tumultuous times with a touch of nostalgia. According to polls, 60 percent of Londoners who survived the Blitz now remember that time as the happiest period of their lives. Somehow a new spirit of community and patriotism sprang up to eclipse even the horror of bombs and V-2 rockets. In the United States, the elderly swap stories about World War II and the Great Depression; they speak fondly of hardships such as blizzards, the childhood outhouse, and the time in college when they ate canned soup and stale bread three weeks in a row.

I ran into this pattern again when I worked on the memoir *(The Gift of Pain)* of Dr. Paul Brand, a missionary surgeon who lived into his ninth decade. As I interviewed him and his wife, Margaret, about their sixty years together, they too kept circling back to the crisis moments.

For example, there was the interval in 1946–47 when Paul had preceded Margaret to Vellore, India. In that year of independence and partition, unrest between Hindus and Muslims began spreading across the northern part of the country. In southern India, though, especially the region around Vellore, Hindus and Muslims lived together in reasonable harmony. Thus Paul wrote and asked his young wife to bring their two infant children and join him as soon as possible.

Back in England, things did not look so rosy. London papers reported that violence was sweeping across India, forcing the greatest human migration in history. Four million refugees had fled to the city of Calcutta alone. In the northwest, Sikhs boarded trains, made men pull down their pants, and killed all those who were circumcised (Muslims); Pakistanis waylaid trains going the opposite direction and killed the uncircumcised (Hindus).

Paul Brand's glowing reports of the situation in Vellore contradicted the frightening headlines Margaret was reading in London: SLAUGHTER IN THE PUNJAB . . . BRINK OF CIVIL WAR . . . MASSACRE OF EUROPEANS PREDICTED. Her family, not realizing the nearest trouble spots were a thousand miles from Vellore, thought it the height of folly for her to take two babies to such a place. But Margaret, trusting her husband, made a leap of faith and did so.

There were other family crises as well, and I have heard versions from both Paul and Margaret. At the time, these dramatic intrusions seemed to call into question their entire relationship. But later they retold the stories with nostalgia, for the crises fit together into—indeed, helped form—a pattern of love and trust. Looking back from the vantage point of sixty years, it seems clear that the Brands' mutual response to the stormy times was what gave their marriage its enduring strength.

Every marriage has crisis times, moments of truth when one partner (or both) is tempted to give up, to judge the other undependable, irrational, untrustworthy. Great marriages survive these moments; weak ones fall apart. When divorce happens, tragically, both partners lose out on the deeper strength that comes only from riding out such stormy times together. If, for example, Margaret Brand had judged her husband crazy for beckoning her to India in the midst of political turmoil and filed for divorce—how sad that would have been. A splendid marriage and partnership in God's work would have been irretrievably lost.

Great relationships take form when they are stretched to the breaking point and do not break. Seeing this principle lived out in people like the Brands, I can better understand one of the mysteries of relating to God. Abraham climbing the hill at Moriah, Job scratching his boils in the hot sun, David hiding in a cave, Elijah moping in a desert, Moses pleading for a new job description—all these heroes experienced crisis moments when they were sorely tempted to judge God uncaring, powerless, or even malign. Confused and in the dark, they faced a turning point: whether to turn away embittered or step forward in faith. In the end, all chose the path of trust, and for this reason we remember them as giants of faith.

The Bible is littered with tales of others—Cain, Samson, Solomon, Judas—who flunked such tests. Their lives, like the marriages that fail too soon, give off a scent of sadness and remorse: oh, what might have been.

In America, I've noticed, a consumer mentality tends to infiltrate relationships as well as commerce. Some people treat marriage partners like automobiles; every few years it's time to upgrade to a new model. Some Christians treat churches the same way. And some even approach God with a consumer spirit: when God performs satisfactorily, he merits our worship, but when God seems distant or unresponsive, why bother?

Why bother? Because the deepest strength comes only through testing.

Partly from listening to elderly people, I have learned that faith means trusting in advance what will make sense only in reverse. Sixty years casts another light on marriage; the century looks different from a grandmother's view. And I believe that human history will take on a new look from the vantage point of eternity. Every scar, every hurt, every disappointment will be seen in a different light, bathed in an eternity of love and trust. Not even the murder of God's own son could end the relationship between God and human beings. In the alchemy of redemption, that most villainous crime became a day we now call Good Friday.

# Chapter 40

# Will God Forgive What I'm About to Do?

Steven Spielberg's film version of *The Color Purple* includes a moving portrayal of a parable of grace. Sugar, a sexy, knock-'em-dead nightclub singer who works out of a ramshackle bar by the side of a river, is the classic prodigal daughter. Her father, a minister who preaches hellfire and brimstone in a church just across the way, hasn't spoken to her in years.

One day as Sug is crooning "I've got somethin' to tell you" in the bar, she hears the church choir answer, as if antiphonally, "God's got something to tell you!" Pricked by nostalgia or guilt, Sug leads her band to the church and marches down the aisle just as her father mounts the pulpit to preach on the prodigal son.

The sight of his long-lost daughter silences the minister, and he glowers at the procession coming down the aisle. "Even us sinners have soul," Sug explains, and hugs her father, who hardly reacts. Ever the moralist, he cannot easily forgive a daughter who has shamed him so.

The Hollywood portrayal, however, altogether misses the main point of the biblical parable. In Jesus' version the father does not glower, but rather searches the horizon, desperate for any sign of his wayward child. It is the father who runs, throws his arm around the prodigal, and kisses him.

By making a sinner the magnanimous hero, Hollywood dodges the scandal of grace. In truth, what blocks forgiveness is not God's reticence—"But while he was still a long way off, his father saw him and was filled with compassion for him"—but ours. God's arms are always extended; we are the ones who turn away. It is a wonderful truth, and one subject to devious exploitation.

Not long ago I sat in a restaurant and listened to yet another variation on a familiar theme. A good friend of mine whom I'll call Daniel confided that he had decided to leave his wife after fifteen years of marriage. He had met someone younger and prettier, someone who "makes me feel alive, like I haven't felt in years."

Daniel, a Christian, knew well the personal and moral consequences of what he was about to do. His decision to leave would inflict permanent damage on his wife and three children. Even so, he said, the force pulling him toward the younger woman was too strong to resist.

I listened to his story with sadness and grief. Then, during the dessert course, he dropped the bombshell. "The reason I wanted to see you tonight was to ask you a question. Do you think God can forgive something as awful as I am about to do?"

Historian and art critic Robert Hughes tells of a convict sentenced to life imprisonment on a maximum security island off the coast of Australia. One day with no provocation, he turned on a fellow prisoner he barely knew and beat him senseless. The murderer was shipped back to the mainland to stand trial, where he gave a straightforward, passionless account of the crime, showing no sign of remorse. "Why?" asked the bewildered judge. "What was your motive?"

The prisoner replied that he was sick of life on the island, a notoriously brutal place, and that he saw no reason to keep on living. "Yes, yes, I understand all that," said the judge. "I can see why you might drown yourself in the ocean. But why murder?"

"Well, it's like this," said the prisoner. "I'm a Catholic. If I commit suicide I'll go straight to Hell. But if I murder, I can come back here and confess to a priest before my execution. That way, God will forgive me."

Do we fully appreciate the *scandal* of unconditional grace? How can I dissuade my friend Daniel from committing a terrible mistake if he knows forgiveness lies just around the corner? Or, worse, why not murder if you know in advance you'll be forgiven?

The scandal of grace must have haunted the apostle Paul as he wrote the Book of Romans. The first three chapters ring down condemnation on every class of human being, concluding, "There is no one righteous, not even one." The next two chapters unveil the miracle of a grace so boundless that, as Paul says, "where sin increased, grace increased all the more."

Paul's tone changes in chapter 6. I can almost see the apostle staring at the papyrus and scratching his head, thinking to himself, *Wait a minute! What have I said?* What's to keep a murderer, adulterer, or common sinner from exploiting God's lavish promise of "forgiveness in advance"?

More than once in the next few chapters, Paul returns to this logical predicament: "What shall we say, then? Shall we go on sinning so that grace may increase?" To such a devious question he has a pithy answer ("By no means!" or, as the King James Version has it, "God forbid!") and a lengthy one. What Paul keeps circling around in those dense, wonderful chapters (6–8) is, quite simply, the scandal of grace.

Here is what I told my friend Daniel, in a nutshell. "Can God forgive you? Of course. Read your Bible. David, Peter, Paul—God builds his church on the backs of people who murder, commit adultery, deny him, and persecute his followers. But because of Christ, forgiveness is now our problem, not God's. What we have to go through to commit sin distances us from God—we change in the very act of rebellion—and there is no guarantee we will come back. You ask me about forgiveness now, but will you even want it later, especially if it involves repentance?"

Several months after our conversation, Daniel made his choice. I have yet to see any evidence of repentance. Now he tends to rationalize his decision as a way of escaping an unhappy marriage. He has rejected most of his Christian friends—"Too narrow-minded," he says—and looks instead for people who celebrate his newfound liberation.

To me, though, Daniel does not seem very liberated. The price of his "freedom" has meant turning his back on those who cared about him most. He also tells me God is not a part of his life right now. "Maybe later," he says.

God took a great risk by announcing forgiveness in advance. It occurs to me, though, that the scandal of grace involves a transfer of that risk to us. As George MacDonald put it, we are condemned not for the wicked things we've done, but for not leaving them.

# Chapter 41

# Holy Secrets

Almost everyone has occasion to wish for an ability to see into the future. *Is this person the one I should marry? Should I accept that new job offer? How will my rebellious son turn out? If only, dear God, I could have a glimpse of the future, a mere clue as to how it will turn out, decisions would be so much simpler.*

What would Abraham Lincoln or Winston Churchill have given for such preternatural vision during their crises of war? What would the CIA pay for certain knowledge of how the Middle East and North Korea will look ten years from now?

As I read the Bible, though, I can begin to understand why God seldom shares inside information about the future. The plain fact is, most human beings cannot handle it.

Take the prophet Balaam, a mysterious Old Testament character who received a series of unmistakable messages from God about the Israelites' future (although it required a talking donkey to overcome his initial resistance). In the end, Balaam failed to heed his own message, working against the very Israelites whose triumph he had predicted. He was finally executed as an enemy of God's people (see Numbers 22–24, 31; Deuteronomy 23).

Or consider Hezekiah. One of Judah's best kings, he received from God an unprecedented extension to his life. But once he learned of those fifteen bonus years, Hezekiah set about squandering them; in the process he sowed the seeds for his nation's downfall and eventual captivity by Babylon (see 2 Kings 18–20; 2 Chronicles 29–32; Isaiah 39).

The classic Old Testament tale of foreknowledge centers on Saul and David. The prophet Samuel delivered a similar announcement to both of them: Saul would lose the kingdom, for God had chosen another to lead the nation. King Saul spent the next decade or so in rebellion against that future, trying desperately to kill the one whom God had designated as his replacement. David, who shared the same foreknowledge, makes a striking contrast. Refusing to take the future into his own hands, he turned down several chances to depose Saul and as a result spent those years hiding out in caves and deserts. The Psalms reveal that he sometimes wondered whether God had forgotten about the plan, but even so David remained faithful (see 1 Samuel 9–31).

In the New Testament, the apostle Paul offers another example of the wise use of foreknowledge. Bad news about the future didn't scare him: he went to Jerusalem despite strong warnings that a visit there would result in his arrest and imprisonment. But good news about the future didn't make him cocky or passive: after learning in a vision that all passengers would survive a shipwreck off Malta, Paul took command, giving instructions to the Roman guards and mobilizing the rescue efforts (see Acts 20–21, 27–28).

These and many other biblical examples make clear that human beings don't easily cope with advance knowledge of the future (Adam and Eve certainly didn't). They are far more likely to respond by either rebelling against bad news, as King Saul and Balaam did, or getting cocky about good news, as Hezekiah did.

I once viewed foreknowledge as a "genie in a bottle" gift of magic that affords the recipient an enviable advantage. I now see it as a rather demanding test of faith. David in exile dreaming of his coronation, Hezekiah debating fifteen-year plans, the apostle Paul riding out a Mediterranean storm, even Jesus praying in Gethsemane—all had special foresight into what end awaited them, but that hardly made the *process* any easier. It takes an extra measure of faith to endure with patience and obedience the long hours or years that precede whatever future you know about in advance. Ask the Old Testament prophets.

Unlike Balaam, Hezekiah, Saul, and David, most of us today do not receive a special revelation as to how our specific future will turn out. (Frankly, as I look back on their lives, I'm glad.) But in at least one instance, all Christians face a test of "responsible foreknowledge." It involves the spectacular good news about God's grace and forgiveness as revealed in Jesus' parables and in such New Testament letters as Romans and Galatians.

"Therefore there is now no condemnation for those who are in Christ Jesus," Paul proclaims in Romans 8. That's about as sweeping a statement as he could make—and far more dangerous than if he had said, "Well, God can't promise anything. There *may* not be any condemnation; it all depends on how you behave from now on." It seems that God the Judge has revealed his merciful verdict even before the trial begins!

Paul seems fully aware that advance knowledge of such all-encompassing good news might be subject to abuse. That is why in Romans 6, after proving that God's grace triumphs over all sin, he interrupts himself to ask the rhetorical question that captures the logic of someone intent on handling foreknowledge irresponsibly: "Shall we go on sinning so that grace may increase?" And why a few paragraphs later he stops again—like a preacher who realizes he's just said something outrageous—and repeats the question.

The scandal of grace—God informing us of our forgiveness *in advance*—is probably the closest most of us will come to certain knowledge of the future. As my friend Daniel showed, that very knowledge opens up all sorts of devious possibilities.

More and more, I have begun to see that Paul's explosive response "God forbid!" is the only appropriate response to human questions about exploiting God's grace. If you're the kind of person who seizes upon God's grace just for the chance to push it to the limits, why, you probably haven't understood that grace at all.

If a bridegroom on his wedding night sat down to negotiate terms of infidelity—"Okay, you've guaranteed the future by promising to stick with me regardless. Just how far can I go with other women? Can I hug them? Kiss them? Go to bed with them? How often? How many?"—we would call such a husband a fraud, a pathologically sick man. If he approaches marriage that way, he will never learn the meaning of true love. And if a Christian approaches forgiveness the same way—"Let's see, God has promised forgiveness in advance. What can I get away with? How far can I push it?"—that Christian will end up equally impoverished. Paul's response says it all: "God forbid!"

I have come to view God's grace as a matter of responsible foreknowledge, not so different from the special revelations granted a few individuals in the Old and New Testaments. We know the future—God's forgiveness—and such advance knowledge presents us with a choice, a challenge of faith. We can set out to exploit God's promises by probing the outer limits of forgiveness. On the other hand, we can live in a spirit of gratitude, secure enough in God's love to follow him faithfully. It was an extravagant risk God took, entrusting us with such holy secrets.

Part Seven

Finding

God

Within

the

Church

# Chapter 42

# The Church Behind Bars

I have always had a strange, intense curiosity about what happens when human beings are pressed to their limits. As a child, I used to read with quiet horror the stories in *Foxe's Book of Martyrs*. Anticommunism was a national sport in the 1950s, and preachers would regale us with tales of Christian martyrs in Russia and China and Albania. I even studied Chinese, and my brother Russian, to prepare for the day our country would surely be overrun. What would happen when my faith was tested to the extreme? Would I cling to Christ or renounce him to save my skin?

Perhaps because of these nagging questions, I took an unusual writing assignment a few years ago. A good friend, Ron Nikkel, invited me to visit some Christians in the prisons of Chile and Peru. South American jails, I knew, would provide an extreme test of faith for anyone. Although conditions have improved now, at the time Chile was viewed as one of the world's worst human rights violators. And jails in Peru also make news headlines, as hundreds of prisoners have died in riots there.

What does a "church" look like among lumpen people such as these: fenced in, ill fed, vulnerable to sexual assaults, sentenced to years of misery among murderers, thieves, rapists, and drug dealers? Can the hope of the gospel survive such conditions? I decided to find out.

I am sitting in the midst of a church service that has a distinctly Latin and Pentecostal flavor. On the platform, a "band" consisting of eighteen guitarists, one accordionist, and two men wielding handmade brass tambourines is leading a rousing rendition of a folksy song called "The Banquet of the Lord."

The congregation, 150 strong, lustily joins in. Some people raise their hands above their heads. Some seem to be competing in a highest-decibel contest. A few hug their neighbors. The meeting room is overflowing, and extra faces are peering in all the windows.

Except for a few visual reminders, I could easily forget that we are meeting in one of the largest prisons in Chile. I look around at the congregation: all men, wearing a ragtag assortment of handed-down street clothes. A shocking number of their faces are marked with scars.

After the singing, a Canadian guest, conspicuous in a white shirt and tie, comes to the platform. The prison chaplain informs the crowd that this man, Ron Nikkel, has visited prisons in more than fifty countries. The organization he directs, Prison Fellowship International, brings the message of Jesus to prisoners and works with governments on improving prison conditions. A dozen inmates yell a loud "Amen!"

"I bring you greetings from your brothers and sisters in Christ in prisons around the world," Ron begins, pausing for the translation into Spanish. He is a broad-shouldered man of moderate height with a freckled face that gives him a youthful look. His soft voice must compete with noise flowing in from the outside— guards blowing whistles, inmates playing basketball in the exercise yard, music blaring from the cell blocks.

"I bring you greetings especially from Pascal, who lives in Africa, in a country called Madagascar. Pascal trained as a scientist and took pride in his atheism. One day he was arrested for participating in a student strike. He was thrown into a prison designed for eight hundred men, but now crowded with twenty-five hundred men. They sat elbow to elbow on bare boards, most of them dressed in rags and covered with lice. You can imagine the sanitation there." The Chilean inmates, who have been listening alertly, groan aloud with sympathy.

"Pascal had only one book available in the prison—a Bible provided by his family. He read it daily and, despite his atheistic beliefs, he began to pray. He found that science could not help him in a prison." (Loud laughter.) "By the end of three months, Pascal was leading a Bible study every night in that crowded room.

"Much to his surprise, Pascal was released after those three months. Someone in the government had a change of heart. But here is an amazing thing: Pascal keeps going back to prison! He visits twice each week to preach and to distribute Bibles. On Fridays he brings in huge pots of vegetable soup, because he found that the prisoners were dying of malnutrition. Many had been jailed for stealing food—they were hungry before they went in!"

The Chileans look around at each other. This story is hitting close. Ron continues.

"Pascal shows the difference Christ can make in a person's life. When you walk out of prison, you'll probably want to erase it from your mind. But Pascal couldn't do that. He believed God wanted him to go back, to share God's love that he had found in that stinking, crowded room."

After the story, the Chilean prisoners, obviously moved, break out in loud applause. Ron continues, telling story after story of people who have met Christ behind bars. Then members of the congregation stand up to speak.

One of the band members, a short, wiry man with a thick scar running across his left cheek, speaks first. "They used to think I was so dangerous that they kept me in chains. And I'll tell you why I first started going to prison church—I was looking for an escape hole!" Everyone laughs, even the guards. "But there I found true freedom in Christ, not just a way to escape."

Another prisoner limps to the front. He explains that he lost a leg and most of his bowels in a shooting incident in an Argentine prison. He became a Christian in 1985, he says. Shortly after that he located the man who had killed his brother. "Before, I would have killed that man," he says. "But with Christ in my heart, I was able to forgive him. Now I know I am called to preach to the others here in prison. It's a more important job than being president of General Motors. And with thirty-four years to go on my sentence, I'll have plenty of time!"

The service goes on, gathering emotional steam. Prisoners spontaneously kneel by the rough wooden benches to pray for their fellow inmates. The singing, animated with hand-clapping and foot-stomping, gets louder and more boisterous. Other prisoners abandon their basketball games and crowd around the open doorway to see what they are missing. When the foreign visitors leave, amid many hugs and handshakes, all the prisoners stay. They are just getting warmed up.

I can still hear strains of the prisoners' singing as I settle with other visitors around a long rectangular table in the prison warden's office. The warden has asked Ron Nikkel and his guests to meet with the prison's psychologist, sociologist, and social workers. Clearly, we are being shown one of Chile's showcase prisons, featuring modern facilities and services.

The staff professionals view the effect of Christian faith on the inmates with a spirit of benign tolerance: sprinkle saltpeter on the inmates' toast to help control their sex drives, and why not add a small dose of religion to help control their tempers. The chaplain and other Prison Fellowship staff members, however, believe their work among inmates can contribute far more. Using statistics and case studies, they try to demonstrate that no rehabilitation scheme will work unless it takes into account the inmates' spiritual needs.

The discussion ranges inconclusively along such lines for thirty minutes, at which time the prison warden crosses a tolerance threshold. In every way, the warden fulfills the perfect Hollywood stereotype of a South American military officer. Only a bushy moustache breaks up the stony monotony of his sallow face. His huge barrel chest serves as a perfect display board for rows and rows of multicolored military ribbons, and his shoulder epaulet sports three stars.

When the warden speaks, everyone else falls silent. "It doesn't matter to me which faith these prisoners take to," he announces with finality. "But it's clear they need to change, and they'll never do it without some outside assistance. Religion may give them the will to change that they could never develop on their own."

As he speaks, we can still hear the prisoners singing in the courtyard chapel. "Chaplain," he continues, "one-third of the men in this facility attend your services. You visit several times a week, but I'm here every day. And I tell you, those men are different. They don't just put on a performance when you come around—they are different from the other prisoners. They have a joy. They share with other prisoners. They care about more than themselves. And so I think we ought to do all we can to help this fine work."

The director's statement promptly ends all discussion. All the prison professionals nod their agreement. As we leave the prison, the worship service is finally breaking up. The prisoners are marching around the exercise yard in twin columns, singing hymns to the beat of drums and tambourines. I look at my watch—two hours have passed since the service began.

The taxi to downtown Santiago takes a long, circuitous route, and as we ride, Ron reflects on his day at the prison. "It never fails to get to me, no matter how many prisons I visit," he says. "To see human beings in such miserable conditions, and yet praising God. In their faces you can see a joy and love like I've encountered nowhere else. I wish some of the dispirited Christians back in North America and Europe could travel with me and see the difference Christ can make in a person's life. God chooses the weak and foolish things of the world to confound the wise and the mighty."

I bring you greetings from your brothers and sisters in Christ in prisons around the world," Ron begins again, in another Chilean prison a day later. This one, shoehorned between buildings in urban Santiago, with an asphalt exercise yard and cell blocks stacked vertically in high-rises, conveys a far more oppressive feeling.

The prison chapel, located in a basement, is especially gloomy. To save on energy costs, prison officials have unscrewed every other fluorescent bulb in the ceiling (even the bulbs are covered by bars). I'm beginning to wonder if prisons are designed by architects competing to produce the world's ugliest buildings. All walls are square, functional, and free of ornamentation. Surfaces consist of rough concrete or smooth iron bars, with no mediating textures like tile, carpet, or wallpaper. Prisons strip human inventions, as they do human beings, to the barest essentials.

"I bring you greetings especially from Dr. Appienda Arthur of Ghana, in West Africa. Dr. Arthur committed no crime. He served as a member of parliament and a close adviser to the president of Ghana until a military coup overthrew that government. Dr. Arthur landed in prison.

"One day soldiers marched Dr. Arthur out into a field, handed him a shovel, and ordered him to dig his own grave. When he had dug deep enough, he was blindfolded, with his arms tied behind his back. He stood in a line with other political prisoners. A volley of shots rang out. The prisoners crumpled to the ground, moaning. Dr. Arthur was sure a bullet had pierced his body. He thought he was dead. But then the soldiers, laughing, removed all the blindfolds. They had fired blanks, playing a cruel joke on the prisoners.

"In that prison Dr. Arthur read the Bible, and also a copy of *Born Again* by Chuck Colson, founder of Prison Fellowship. He was moved by the story of a man who, like him, had fallen from power and served time in jail. He knelt on the concrete floor of the prison and promised God he would spend the rest of his life serving God. Dr. Arthur made his way to Fuller Seminary in the U.S., where he studied the Bible. He could have gotten political asylum and stayed there. But instead he decided to return to Africa, to *Ghana*, the country that had almost killed him, in order to serve Christ.

"You can find Dr. Appienda Arthur back in prison today. But he's there voluntarily, as a free man. Dr. Arthur now directs the work of Prison Fellowship in Ghana, bringing the message of Christ to the prisoners there."

By now the Chilean inmates are nodding and interjecting "Amen!" and "Hallelujah!" Ron goes on.

"And I bring you greetings from Jose, a Filipino man I met in a Saudi Arabian jail. He was arrested for murder and has spent the last five years in prison. The police tortured a confession out of him. He later recanted it in court, but he was convicted anyway and will probably face execution.

"Yet Jose found Christ in that Muslim jail, through a Christian cellmate. I visited his prison, a brick building with very little ventilation. It must have been 110 degrees in there. Jose had to shout his testimony to me—visitors must sit in an area four feet away from the prisoners, who are locked in cages covered with double steel mesh. 'My time in here is hell,' Jose yelled. 'But I wouldn't trade it for anything. In this place I met Jesus!' "

As the chapel service continues, the military director of the prison motions for us to follow him. We get a hurried tour of the dreary facility through an endless maze of tunnels and iron gates. Two things stand out: the odor of a forty-year buildup of disinfectant, and the large framed faces of Chile's rulers glowering at us from many walls.

Nothing has prepared me for the director of the oldest prison in Chile. If yesterday's director was straight out of central casting, this one must be on loan from *Saturday Night Live*. He is short and thin with an unruly shock of dark brown hair. Wearing a rumpled green uniform devoid of badges, ribbons, and stars, he dashes around his office in a whirlwind, arranging chairs, showing off his display case collection of swords and knives, making little jokes. His eyebrows dance up and down as he talks, adding punctuation marks to his sentences. In facial expression and mannerisms, he reminds me of Pancho, sidekick of the Cisco Kid.

The director apologizes for a shortage of coffee cups. "I only have three," he says, winking. "Drink fast, and then I'll rinse out the cups and serve the other guests." As Ron Nikkel begins to explain Prison Fellowship to him, this funny man suddenly raises his hand to interrupt. "Ah, but we must have music!" he says. "Do you like disco music, my friends?" He rushes to an oversized white plastic cassette player with the brand name Disco Robo. A Latin rumba beat fills the room, and the director returns to his desk with a broad smile, motioning for Ron to continue.

It is a scene straight out of Kafka. At that time human rights organizations are ranking Chilean prisons near the bottom of the scale; routinely prisoners go on hunger strikes for more humane conditions. And yet we sit in the director's office at one of those prisons, juggling coffee cups and tapping our toes to rumba music.

The ironies carry over into the evening. We eat dinner in one of Santiago's finest restaurants, as the guests of a wealthy man con-

cerned about prison ministry in Chile. Around the table sit Prison
Fellowship staff members, the local board, and several representatives from the government. The restaurant presents a floor show
based on Easter Island themes, and soon the stage is alive with
beautiful women dressed in brightly colored skirts and coconut-
husk tops. Shouting through translators over the din, we try to
discuss prison policy.

I think of a chapter in *The Oak and the Calf*, in which Alexander Solzhenitsyn describes a visit to the Moscow offices of the gulag administration. He has now become famous, and there, in the
plush surroundings of that office, swilling vodka with his genteel,
affable hosts, Solzhenitsyn can barely recall the terrors of his life as
a prisoner in the gulag. His friends still in prison seem very far
away.

"Sometimes I feel like a commuter," Ron Nikkel says to me the
next day. "Only I commute in and out of other people's pain.
Yesterday we spent the morning inside a prison full of agony.
Then we dined with the men who control those prisons. That
paradox tears me apart. I return home after every trip drained and
perplexed. How can we work both with the oppressors and the
oppressed? That's my real dilemma."

Ron likes to cite Winston Churchill's observation that a civilization can be measured by the way it treats its prisoners. Prisons
are the garbage heaps of society. Just as you can learn about the
lives of apartment dwellers by sifting through their garbage cans,
you can sift through a nation's prisons and learn about the larger
society. The United States, for example, has a higher percentage of
prisoners than any other nation. Its prisons demonstrate that freedom and a land of plenty are not enough to meet human needs.

Ironically, Ron sees the utter failure of penal systems around
the world as Prison Fellowship's greatest boon. "If I were to write
a book about the strategy of Prison Fellowship, I would title it

*Holy Subversion*," he says. "Can we subvert the world's powers by working with their rejects, the prisoners?

"Marxists fail at their prisons, as do Muslims, Hindus, and secular humanists. Nothing works. Societies shut prisoners out of sight because they're an embarrassment, an admission of failure. But they let prison ministries in, figuring we can't worsen an already hopeless situation. And there, behind those bars in the least likely of all places, the church of God takes shape.

"It's a New Testament church in its purest form. In Chile, for example, there are five thousand different denominations and church groups! But in Chilean prisons, the Christians are one. Prison abolishes all the normal distinctions of denomination and race and class.

"I cannot give details on some of the most exciting frontiers. I can only say that in societies so closed that they apply the death penalty for a conversion to Christianity, prisons are opening doors to us. Authorities are allowing us to conduct seminars and distribute Bibles. Nothing else has worked in those prisons, so in desperation they turn to the Christians. And even in decadent Western Europe the church is showing signs of life—the church behind bars, that is."

We don't read about such works of God in popular magazines. They report mostly on controversies within the church: scandals among evangelicals, killings of abortion doctors, protests against the pope. But something else is taking place at the grassroots level—below the grassroots level even in societies' dumping grounds. In Northern Ireland, former IRA terrorists now take Communion alongside Protestants they had once sworn to kill. In Papua, New Guinea, prison ministry is led by a judge who used to sentence people to the jails he now visits in the name of Christ.

Bishop Desmond Tutu has said the Western world would experience a "spiritual bankruptcy" if it were deprived of the "moral capital" of its prisoners. He should know: some of his friends, distinguished spokesmen for black South Africa, have spent much of their lives behind bars. Tutu links them to a lineage that includes John Bunyan, Mahatma Gandhi, Martin Luther King, Alexander Solzhenitsyn, and Fyodor Dostoyevsky.

We easily forget that prisons around the world are populated not only by true "criminals," but also by people who happen to hold dissident political opinions. They are serving time for what they *think,* and those same people use their time in prison to refine their political philosophies. Vladimir Lenin, Adolf Hitler, Fidel Castro, Che Guevara, Menachem Begin, Anwar Sadat, François Mitterrand, Helmut Schmidt, and Nelson Mandela all credit their prison experiences with helping to form their outlooks.

Thus, one by-product of prison ministries is the remarkable opportunity to minister to the future leaders of the world. The most spectacular recent result of this "by-product" ministry occurred in the Philippines in the late 1970s, when the leading opposition spokesman, Benigno Aquino, was languishing in prison. Full of anger and bitterness against the Marcos regime, he used his time to study Marxism.

"The guards used to let the dogs eat half my dinner and then give me what was left," Aquino recalled. "I hated everyone." Then his mother sent a copy of Chuck Colson's book *Born Again,* and Aquino found himself strangely moved by the story so full of hope. He became a Christian, and because of that hope was able to survive in prison. It was there that he developed his philosophy of nonviolent revolution.

Unexpectedly, Aquino gained his freedom in 1980, when President Marcos permitted him to travel to the U.S. for heart surgery. While there he met Colson, by coincidence, on an airplane. Colson recalls the incident: "I noticed this Asian man staring at me, and then he grabbed my arm. 'You're Chuck Colson! Your book changed my life.' I'll never forget our conversation.

Benigno told me, 'One day I will go back to the Philippines—either to serve the government or to return to prison. Either way, we'll start Prison Fellowship there. I promised that to the Lord when I walked out of prison.' "

Before leaving, Aquino studied the life of Dietrich Bonhoeffer, who returned to Germany during World War II in full awareness of the dangers. Aquino, of course, never made it past the tarmac in the Philippines. He was shot by the military as he emerged from the door of the plane. But his promise has been fulfilled. Two and a half years later, the nonviolent revolution he had set in motion swept Marcos from power. And Prison Fellowship in the Philippines is now thriving.

I bring you greetings from your brothers and sisters in Christ in prisons around the world," Ron Nikkel says once more, to another group of prisoners. We are in Peru now, and the international travel, combined with long evening meetings with prison volunteers and embassy staff and penal authorities, has taken its toll. Ron's face wears the fatigue of the past week.

Our meeting room adjoins a row of cells, so that in addition to the sixty prisoners in our room, a few others are diffidently watching the proceedings from their beds. In prison, you learn to live with certain things: congestion, constant background noise, ever-glowing light bulbs, an utter lack of privacy. Peru's prisons are advanced enough to have a commode in each cell—it sits in the center of the cell, visible from all sides.

The prisoners in our meeting room are mostly wearing gym shorts, flip-flops, and a comical assortment of T-shirts. While Ron is being introduced, I take visual inventory of some of the T-shirt messages. "Mailmen do it with zip." "Somebody in Utah loves me." "Laguna Beach Country Club." Not even the barbed wire of a Third World prison can keep out American sloganeering.

Today, Ron keeps the stories short. He feels like preaching a sermon. "Did you know that Jesus Christ was a prisoner?" he asks the scruffy-looking group. From their facial expressions, it appears that, no, they did not know that. "Well, he was. Jesus came to earth so that God could experience all that we experience here, and that included going to prison.

"Do you know what it's like when someone squeals on you—turns you in to the authorities?" Vigorous affirmative nods. "Jesus felt that, too. One of his best friends turned him in on a trumped-up charge. Justice was no better in his day than in ours. The government broke all the rules during his trial and sentenced him to death.

"And when he died on the cross, a prisoner died on each side of him. One prisoner taunted him: 'If you're really the Christ, get us out of here!' I've talked to many prisoners who have exactly that same attitude toward God. Some of you may be *angry* at God. You won't listen to him unless he gets you out. But the prisoner on the other cross had a different spirit. He said simply, 'Jesus, I'm guilty but you're innocent. Please remember me.'

"And, listen—only one person in the Bible receives a direct promise of Heaven. It's a thief who lived a life of crime, who did not get baptized, and who probably never went to church. He died within hours after accepting Christ. Yet that thief lives in Heaven today. Jesus guaranteed it."

Ron is warming to his audience, using hand motions, speaking with more force. The tiredness has drained away. He's preaching like a black Southern preacher now, stating a Bible story in simple terms, then embellishing it. "Sometimes when I ask a person to go with me into a prison as a volunteer, they'll say, 'No, Ron, I'm scared. I don't like hanging around thieves and murderers.' If they really feel that way, then they had better not go to Heaven, because I know of at least one thief who will be there, and a few murderers, too!"

The prisoners are eating it up. Ron goes through the Bible telling prison stories. A verse that speaks of the newness of life for

Christians, 2 Corinthians 5:17, is written out on an oily, makeshift blackboard behind Ron, and he points to it. He tells of the apostle Paul and his long nights in jail. "Paul's favorite description of himself is 'a prisoner of Jesus Christ.' But how could Paul write those words about becoming a new creature when he spent so much time in rotten Roman dungeons?" Ron reads from some of Paul's prison letters—bright words, happy words. "They could keep Paul's body under lock and key," he says, "but his soul was free."

After half an hour of preaching to an increasingly receptive audience, Ron turns the meeting back over to the prisoners. Many of them come to the front and tell of the difference Christ has made in their lives. Judging by the prisoners' reactions, the biggest surprise is Juan. Leaning on the shoulder of a woman volunteer named Marie, Juan limps forward to tell his story. The other inmates know him well, for Juan has a reputation as a troublemaker. He limps because of a run-in with prison guards. He assaulted one of the guards, and other guards gave him a beating that broke his hand, bruised his face, and left him partially lame.

Juan speaks in a husky voice. The very act of speaking causes him great pain, and he explains why. While in solitary confinement after the beating, he somehow obtained a can of DDT insecticide and swallowed it. Guards found him in his cell, near death. After that dark night, Marie, a volunteer, began visiting Juan on a special mission: she wanted to give him a reason to live.

Marie suddenly interrupts Juan's story to explain that she herself is living on borrowed time—doctors have discovered an inoperable tumor in her stomach. She points to the kerchief wrapped around her head; radiation caused most of her hair to fall out.

She told Juan in the hospital room, "How dare you take your life when I would do anything to stay alive! You have no right—your life belongs to God." Through her witness, Juan became a Christian.

As Juan and Marie finish their stories, Juan asks the sixty men around him for help in the days ahead. Other inmates will surely scoff at his conversion. The group kneels together to pray for the healing of Juan's body and the strengthening of his faith through difficult times ahead. And as they pray, a warden leads Ron and the rest of our visiting group to another circle of sixty men awaiting us in a different cell block.

Late that afternoon, as we sit in a taxi in Lima's rush-hour traffic, I ask Ron about his sermon. I have known Ron for twenty years, and I would never have expected from him such a sermon. Ron always had a cynical edge to him. Like many of his generation, he bore scars of fundamentalism that made him tentative, skeptical. I ask him what has changed.

"I came to this job with professional training in criminology, and of course I still try to incorporate everything I learned. But I have gradually become convinced that the lasting answer to prison problems is not rehabilitation, but transformation. Initially I hesitated to use phrases like 'Christ is the answer,' but, frankly, I've seen that phrase proved true. I learned certain words in childhood, but the prisoners themselves finally gave meaning to those words. They proved the reality of a theology that had been little more than a mental exercise for me. They showed me faith at its most basic—the opposite of the kind of health-and-wealth theology you hear in North America.

"Jesus calls blessed those who are poor, who weep, who feel hunger, who are hated and excluded and insulted by men. That's a perfect description of many prisoners I know. But can they really be blessed, happy? To my surprise, the answer is yes. Something about the condition of severe human need makes them receptive to the grace of God. They turn to God, and they are filled. It was no accident that John Bunyan wrote *Grace Abounding unto the Chief of Sinners* while in prison.

"The very best rehabilitation programs can only offer a future hope, that life may change when the prisoners get out. Christ offers a future hope—even for those who face the death sentence—and also a present hope. He can give meaning to a life even if it must be spent in an oppressive prison. I've seen it happen too many times to doubt it."

The computer industry has a phrase called the "table-top test." Engineers design wonderful new products: circuit boards, CD-ROM drives, optical scanners. But the real question is, will that new product survive actual use by consumers? What will happen if it accidentally gets pushed off a table? Will it survive? For Ron, prisons have become the table-top test of the Christian faith. There, simple, tough faith is put to the test every day—by people like Juan, the Peruvian man who turned to Christ after his suicide attempt failed. The eternal truth of the gospel will be tested in his life over the next few weeks.

Some people try to prove the truth of the gospel in the halls of academia, battling over apologetics and theology. Others compare the size and force of Christianity against other great religions of the world. Ron Nikkel says he just keeps going to prisons. There he finds the final testing area for forgiveness and love and grace. There he finds whether Christ really is alive.

I ask Ron to think back to the worst setting he'd ever seen. I took this writing assignment to see how faith survives among people who are pressed to the limits. In the dismal prisons we had visited in Chile and Peru, who could dispute the joy we had found among inmates there? But did the pattern hold true around the world? Had he ever found a place of absolute despair, with no crack of hope? What was the ultimate "table-top test" of the gospel?

Ron thought for a moment and then told me about the time he and Chuck Colson visited a maximum security prison in Zambia. Their "guide," a former prisoner named Nego, had described a secret inner prison built inside to hold the very worst offenders.

To Nego's amazement, one of the guards agreed to let him show the facility to Chuck and Ron.

"We approached a steel cagelike building covered with wire mesh. Cells lined the outside of the cage, surrounding a 'courtyard' fifteen by forty feet. Twenty-three hours of each day the prisoners are kept in cells so small that they cannot all lie down at once. For one hour they are allowed to walk around in the small courtyard. Nego had spent twelve years in those cells.

"When we approached the inner prison, we could see sets of eyes peering at us from a two-inch space under the steel gate. And when the gate swung open, it revealed squalor unlike anything I have seen anywhere. There were no sanitation facilities—in fact, the prisoners were forced to defecate in their food pans. The blazing African sun had heated up the steel enclosure unbearably. I could hardly breathe in the foul, stifling atmosphere of that place. How could human beings possibly live in such a place, I wondered.

"And yet, here is what happened when Nego told them who we were. Eighty of the 120 prisoners went to the back wall and assembled in rows. At a given signal, they began singing—hymns, Christian hymns, in beautiful four-part harmony. Nego whispered to me that thirty-five of those men had been sentenced to death and would soon face execution.

"I was overwhelmed by the contrast between their peaceful, serene faces and the horror of their surroundings. Just behind them, in the darkness, I could make out an elaborate charcoal sketch drawn on the wall. It showed Jesus, stretched out on a cross. The prisoners must have spent hours working on it. And it struck me with great force, the force of revelation, that Christ was there with them, sharing their suffering, and giving them joy enough to sing in such a place.

"I was supposed to speak to them, to offer some inspiring words of faith. But I could only mumble a few words of greeting. *They* were the teachers, not I."

# Chapter 43

# Two-Handed Faith

I have gained fresh insight into the meaning of faith from an unlikely combination of sources: the writings of political dissidents and an eighteenth-century French mystic.

For many years dissidents in Eastern Europe lived under oppressive regimes that tended to promote a sense of paranoia. As the saying goes, "Just because you're paranoid doesn't mean they're not after you," and these dissidents responded appropriately. They met in secret, used code words, avoided public telephones, and published pseudonymous essays in underground papers.

In the mid-seventies, however, Polish and Czech intellectuals began to realize that the constant double life had cost them dearly. Quite simply, they had lost the most basic sense of freedom and human dignity. By working in secret, always with a nervous glance over the shoulder, they had succumbed to fear, the goal of their communist opponents all along. They made a conscious decision to change tactics.

"We will act as if we are free, at all costs," the Poles, and then the Czechs, decided. The Workers' Defense Committee in Poland began holding public meetings, often in church buildings, despite the presence of known informers. They signed articles, sometimes adding an address and phone number, and distributed newspapers openly on street corners.

In effect, the dissidents agreed to start acting in the way they thought society should become. If you want freedom of speech, speak freely. If you want an open society, act openly. If you love the truth, tell the truth. Vaclav Havel, the Czech playwright and future president, led the way by determining to write no longer with an eye on what the authorities might approve, but to write the truth, no matter what.

The authorities did not know how to respond. Sometimes they cracked down—nearly all the dissidents spent time in prison—and sometimes they watched with a frustration bordering on helplessness. Meanwhile the dissidents' brazen tactics made it far easier for them to connect with one another and the West, and a kind of "freedom archipelago" took shape, a bright counterpart to the darkling gulag archipelago. In a sense, they created a free society by acting "as if" their society was free.

Over time, the new approach emboldened the dissidents themselves; they discovered that inner freedom gives sustenance even when external freedom is snatched away. Prison, after all, provides an ideal setting in which to learn to cherish freedom. Against all odds, they clung to belief in fundamental principles of truth and justice even as their governments tried to compel them to believe the opposite.

The daring philosophy spread to other places, giving courage to dissidents in China, Latin America, and South Africa. As

Richard Steele wrote about his experience in a South African prison:

> The *power* of fearlessness is astonishing. I think of those who
> were giving me orders. They were under a real tyranny and
> far more the victim of it than I was. When they were
> yelling their orders at me, I had a vivid image of these tiny
> creatures assaulting my feet, wanting to demolish me with
> orders, while I was way above, not on their level at all.
> They could threaten me with anything at all and not get
> me, because I wasn't afraid. This was immensely liberating
> to me. I could be the person I was without fearing them.
> They had no power over me.

Remarkably, we have lived to see these dissidents triumph. An alternative kingdom of people united by ideas, a kingdom of rags, of prisoners, of poets and philosophers who convey their words in the scrawl of hand-copied samizdat, has toppled what seemed an impregnable fortress in country after country. Even South Africa held free elections and abolished apartheid without a violent revolution.

I vividly remember watching television news reports as the climactic nonviolent revolution took place in the streets of Moscow. Russians who had grown up in the world center of totalitarianism suddenly declared, "We will act as if we are free"—in front of the KGB building, staring down the mouths of tank cannons. I was traveling in Scandinavia that summer, and as I watched the images, lacking an English translation, I could only guess at the details of what was transpiring just across the border. The contrast between the faces of the leaders inside and the masses outside told me all I needed to know, though. With startling clarity, they showed who was really afraid, and who was really free.

On this same trip I read *The Sacrament of the Present Moment*, a remarkable book by the French mystic Jean-Pierre de Caussade, translated by Kitty Muggeridge. Writing to a group of beleaguered nuns in the chaotic decades before the French Revolution, he set out for them a challenging program of spiritual direction.

"Faith gives the whole earth a celestial aspect," said de Caussade. "Each moment is a revelation of God." Regardless of how things appear at a given moment in time, all of history will ultimately serve to accomplish God's purpose on earth. He advised the nuns to "love and accept the present moment as the best, with perfect trust in God's universal goodness. . . . Everything without exception is an instrument and means of sanctification."

Objections immediately sprang to my mind, as probably happened with the nuns who first read those words. "God's universal goodness" in a nation careering toward blood and madness? "A celestial aspect" in a world growing increasingly pagan? Suffering, violence, persecution—are these too instruments and means of sanctification?

Watching newsreels from Red Square on Finnish television, reading the hard words from de Caussade, I came up with a new definition of faith: paranoia in reverse.

A truly paranoid person organizes his or her life around a common perspective of fear. Whatever happens feeds that fear. Try to comfort a paranoiac, "I'm here to help you, not hurt you," and you will merely increase the fear. (Of course he'd say that—he's part of the conspiracy.)

Faith works in the reverse manner. A faithful person organizes his or her life around a common perspective of trust, not fear. Bedrock faith convinces me that despite the apparent chaos of the present moment, God does reign; that regardless of how cast off I may feel, I matter, truly matter, to a God of love; that no pain lasts forever and no evil triumphs in the end. Faith sees even the darkest deed of all history, the death of God's Son, as a necessary prelude to the brightest. Faith allows me to live under the reign of

God even on a planet ruled by a sinister force known as "the god of this world."

Centuries ago Gregory of Nicea called Saint Basil's faith *ambidextrous* because he welcomed pleasures with the right hand and afflictions with the left, convinced that both would serve God's design for him. "God's purpose for us is always what will contribute most to our good," said de Caussade. Tough words. I believe them today, but will I tomorrow?

We have seen in our own time what can happen when a group of people band together to live out a truth—*we are free*—that all around them is being denounced as a lie. Walls and kingdoms crumble. What would happen if we in God's kingdom *acted as if* the words of the apostle John are literally true: "The one who is in you is greater than the one who is in the world"? What would happen if we started living *as if* the most-repeated prayer in Christendom has actually been answered, that God's will be done on earth as it is in heaven?

# Chapter 44

# Don't Forget to Laugh

The human species is distinctive in at least three ways, said poet W. H. Auden. We are the only animals that work, laugh, and pray. I have found that Auden's list provides a neat framework for self-reflection. What about Christians who live in relative freedom, security, and comfort, I wonder. If indeed faith can transform the lives of those pressed to the edge of human endurance, what about the rest of us? How do we measure up?

At *work*, Christians unabashedly excel. In Latin America, Islamic countries, and even Communist China, opponents must grudgingly acknowledge that for all their faults, Christians are industrious. Our forefathers invented the Protestant work ethic, after all.

We value the work ethic so highly, in fact, that we let it gobble everything in sight. Our churches are run like corporations, our quiet times fit into a Day-Timer schedule (ideally on computer software), our pastors maintain the hectic pace of Japanese executives. Work has become for Christians the only sanctioned addiction.

The art of *prayer* we should have mastered by now, but I have my doubts. It is tempting to turn prayer into another form of work, which may explain why prayers in most churches consist mainly of intercession. We bring God our requests in the form of wish lists, and all too rarely do we get around to listening.

I've noticed that biblical prayers (as seen, for example, in the Psalms) tend to be wandering, repetitive, and unstructured—closer in form to the conversation you might hear in a barber shop than a shopping list. I am learning about such prayer from the Catholics, who have a better grasp on prayer as an act of worship. Oddly, for those who do it all day—Henri Nouwen, Thomas Merton, Macrina Wiederkehr, Gerard Manley Hopkins, Teresa of Ávila—prayer seems less like a chore and more like a never-ending conversation. Like ordinary life with the simple addition of an Audience.

I recall an interview Dan Rather did with Mother Teresa of Calcutta. "What do you say to God when you pray?" he asked. Mother Teresa looked at him with her dark, soulful eyes and said quietly, "I listen." Slightly flustered, Rather tried again. "Well, then, what does God say?" Mother Teresa smiled. "He listens."

In *laughter,* the third leg of Auden's triad, Christians trail behind the rest of the world. How else to explain the low circulation of a humor magazine like the *Wittenberg Door* and the angry letters Christian magazines receive from subscribers who fail to comprehend satire?

To correct the imbalance, W. H. Auden proposed resurrecting the medieval practice of Carnival, the raucous holiday preceding Lent. He writes, "Carnival celebrates the unity of our human race as mortal creatures, who come into this world and depart from it without our consent, who must eat, drink, defecate, belch, and break wind in order to live, and procreate if our species is to survive. Our feelings about this are ambiguous. . . . We oscillate between wishing we were unreflective animals and wishing we were disembodied spirits, for in either case we should not be problematic to ourselves. The Carnival solution of this ambiguity is to laugh, for laughter is simultaneously a protest and an acceptance."

In the Middle Ages, Carnival offered an outlet for expressing such ambiguity. Young men dressed up as girls, young women as boys. Individuals hid behind masks and costumes that tended to caricature the oddity of the human animal through exaggeration and parody: false noses, elaborate hairdos, skulls, fat bellies, fanged teeth, horns.

I got caught in Mardi Gras once, smack in the middle of Bourbon Street, New Orleans, and I must say it bore little resemblance to the medieval Carnival. Young women walked through the streets yelling, "Breasts for beads!" In exchange for a gaudy plastic necklace they'd pull up their T-shirts and bare themselves. In their drunkenness, lust, and even violence, the revelers at Mardi Gras were not parodying but rather groveling in their animalness.

The descent from the church's Carnival to the debauchery of Mardi Gras is a theological descent. As G. K. Chesterton put it, "If it is not true that a divine being fell, then one can only say that one of the animals went completely off its head." That, precisely, is where Christians part company with modern materialists. Carnival parodies a divine being who fell; Mardi Gras celebrates an animal gone completely off its head.

C. S. Lewis once said that in the absence of any other evidence, the essentials of natural theology could be argued from the human phenomena of dirty jokes and attitudes toward death. Dirty jokes dwell almost exclusively on the subjects of excretion and reproduction, two of the most "natural" processes on earth;

yet in our smirks and double entendres we treat them as utterly unnatural, even comical. Try to envision a horse or cow bashful about the need to excrete in public. Or imagine a dog or cat with sexual hangups, reluctant to mate. Functions that we share with all other animals somehow, to humans alone, seem strange. Similarly, the only good reason to find humor in such phenomena as over-sized noses and the belching reflex is that we still retain the faintest echo of Eden. In some deep and ambiguous manner of instinct, it seems odd to us that we upright vertebrates, tipped with a divine flame, act so much like other vertebrates.

As for death, only we humans treat it with shock and revulsion, as though we can't get used to the reality, universal though it may be. Every culture devises elaborate ceremonies to mark the final passage of a human being. Even those of us in the Christian West, with our traditional belief in an afterlife, dress up our corpses in new suits, embalm them (for what, posterity?) and bury them in airtight caskets and concrete vaults. In these rituals we act out a stubborn reluctance to yield to this most powerful of human experiences. As Lewis suggests, these anomalies betray a permanent state of tension within human beings. An individual person is a spirit made in the image of God but merged for a time with a body of flesh, and dirty jokes and an obsession with death express a rumbling sense of discord about this in-between state. We lack unity because long ago a gap fissured open between our mortal and immortal parts; theologians trace the fault line back to the Fall.

Christians have a great advantage over other people, C. S. Lewis continued: not by being less fallen than they nor less doomed to live in a fallen world, but by knowing that they are fallen creatures in a fallen world. For this reason, I think, we dare not forget how to laugh at ourselves. I have read some of the classical materialists—Charles Darwin, Karl Marx, and Bertrand Russell—and I have yet to find the slightest curve of a smile lurking among their words. The "politically correct" movement of our time shows a similar solemnity. One can parody only what one respects, just as one can blaspheme only if one believes.

It occurs to me, in fact, that laughter has much in common with prayer. In both acts, we stand on equal ground, freely acknowledging ourselves as fallen creatures. We take ourselves less seriously. We think of our creatureliness. Work divides and ranks; laughter and prayer unite.

W. H. Auden ends his reflection with this warning: "A satisfactory human life, individually or collectively, is possible only if proper respect is paid to all three worlds. Without Prayer and Work, the Carnival laughter turns ugly, the comic obscenities grubby and pornographic, the mock aggression into real hatred and cruelty. Without Laughter and Work, Prayer turns Gnostic, cranky, Pharisaic, while those who try to live by Work alone, without Laughter or Prayer, turn into insane lovers of power, tyrants who would enslave Nature to their immediate desire—an attempt which can only end in utter catastrophe, shipwreck on the Isle of the Sirens."

# Chapter 45

# Saints and Semi-Saints

The biblical characters Ezra and Nehemiah, exact contemporaries, faced the same leadership challenge. Each sought to revive dispirited refugees in Jerusalem by persuading them to rebuild city walls and clean up their morals. But what different tactics the two men used!

When Ezra arrived in Jerusalem and saw firsthand the moral degeneration of his people, he went into a state of shock. He tore his clothes, yanked hair from his head and beard, and sat down appalled. Hours later, Ezra was still weeping and throwing himself on the ground. So demonstrative was his grief and so infectious his repentance that the city leaders all agreed to change their ways.

Nehemiah, who arrived on the scene a few years later, used a more confrontational approach. As merchants lined up outside the city to sell goods on the Sabbath, he threatened them with physical violence. And when fellow Jews married foreigners against

God's command, he called down curses on them, beat them, and pulled out their hair.

That last scene highlights the difference between the two biblical heroes: one pulls out his own hair in grief; another pulls out other people's hair in anger.

Ezra was a priest, a mystic. He had refused an armed escort for the eight-hundred-mile journey from Babylon to Jerusalem despite the fact that his group of émigrés carried twenty-eight tons of silver. Concerned that the presence of armed guards might demonstrate a lack of faith, he chose to rely instead on fasting and prayer for protection.

Nehemiah, a bureaucrat of exquisite pragmatism, had no such scruples. He entered Jerusalem at the head of a Persian cavalry detachment, and at the first sign of opposition he organized the Jews, too, into armed battalions. Soon every workman on the wall was carrying a weapon in his free hand.

Ezra and Nehemiah got me thinking about the different approaches people take in living out their Christian faith. If Ezra was a saint, Nehemiah was a semi-saint.

A *saint* (as I am using the term) is a radical, a moral extremist who shuns all compromise and may well look foolish in the eyes of the world. Mother Teresa stood in the center of one of the most crowded cities on earth and lectured against birth control. "Every baby is a gift from God," she said. Forty years ago, Martin Luther King Jr. would seek out the meanest sheriffs in Alabama and Mississippi and plant his unarmed body directly in the path of their dogs and fire hoses. His goal, King used to say, was not to defeat the white man, but "to awaken a sense of shame within the oppressor," and the best way to shame a nation was to fight violence with aggressive nonviolence.

The church has seen some effective *semi-saints* as well. William

Wilberforce became the butt of many jokes in eighteenth-century England because of his one-note-band speeches in Parliament against slavery. But in the end, his bureaucratic faithfulness helped carry the day, and England chose the way of moral courage, even agreeing to compensate slave owners in the colonies. In our own country, Abraham Lincoln believed, truly believed, that he would serve God best by pursuing a terrible war to its bitter end.

My writing career has afforded me the chance to observe a few contemporary "saints." Some have left comfortable homes in North America to witness for peace in Central America or to serve in squalid refugee camps in Africa; others spend their lives sheltering and feeding America's urban homeless. After talking to these people, I go away inspired, ennobled, and filled with a higher vision of what a Christian can be.

I have also met some semi-saints. Every working day, Christian lobbyists put on three-piece suits and traipse over to Capitol Hill to represent the interests of starving children and aborted babies and maltreated prisoners and victims of human rights abuses. These semi-saints may play a less glamorous role, but can anyone doubt that an organization like Bread for the World accomplishes as much on behalf of the poor and hungry?

In India today some "holy men" are leading a campaign against deforestation. These visionaries encourage villagers to tie themselves to trees in order to block the loggers and their chain saws. Television crews flock to cover the dramatic scene of protest (a cause that I, for one, support). But the saintly protest in India might not even be necessary if every semi-saint in America would diligently recycle envelopes and daily newspapers.

Although we need saints, desperately, they will probably always be a rare breed. The vast majority of Christians in this country work at "secular" jobs from nine to five each day, worship on Sundays, and try to let their faith influence their lives. Such folks may never enjoy the singular vision, or perhaps the freedom from ambiguity, that characterizes a genuine saint. But I take comfort in the fact that the Bible seems to allow for both approaches.

Ezra and Nehemiah, telling the same story from two points of view, make clear that neither approach is entirely effective on its own. Nehemiah, the obsessive, management-oriented bureaucrat, completed in fifty-two days a mission that Ezra had failed to accomplish in a dozen years: he got a wall built around Jerusalem to provide security for the residents inside.

On the other hand, once the construction project was completed, Nehemiah turned to Ezra to lead the religious celebration. The latter part of Nehemiah depicts that day as one of the most remarkable scenes of Old Testament history. A vast throng of refugees assembled in a huge plaza, and Ezra read from the Law from daybreak until noon. Working in tandem, the two leaders—Nehemiah with his no-nonsense pragmatism and Ezra with his unimpeachable integrity—directed a spiritual revival such as had not been seen in a thousand years. In that revival, both saints and semi-saints played a part.

Chapter 46

# In Search of a
# Both/And Church

Not long ago I attended a conference held on the restored grounds of a century-old Utopian community in Indiana. As I ran my fingers over the fine workmanship of the buildings and read the plaques describing the daily lives of the true believers, I marveled at the energy that drove this movement, one of dozens spawned by American idealism and religious fervor.

Many varieties of perfectionism have grown on American soil: offshoots from the Second Great Awakening, the Victorious Life movement, communes of the Jesus movement. It occurred to me, though, that in recent times the perfectionist urge has virtually disappeared. Nowadays we tilt in the opposite direction, toward a kind of anti-Utopianism. For example, as a result of the recovery movement, many churches have formed twelve-step groups around the theme of addiction to sex, food, alcohol, or drugs; these groups by definition center on members' *inability* to be perfect.

I confess my preference for this modern trend. I observe far more proofs of human fallibility than perfectibility, and I have cast my lot with a gospel based on grace. Yet in New Harmony, Indiana, I felt an unaccountable nostalgia for the Utopians: all those solemn figures in black clothes breaking rocks in the fields, devising ever-stricter rules in an attempt to rein in lust and greed, striving to fulfill the lofty commands of the New Testament. The mere names they left behind are enough to break your heart: New Harmony, Peace Dale, New Hope, New Haven.

The Catholic Church has bred its share of perfectionism as well. I have studied the rule of Saint Benedict and read the stirring accounts of early Jesuit missionaries who sailed to Japan and China. Compared with such discipline and dedication, the current wave of short-term missions seems like a consumer fad. What will we moderns leave behind for future generations to ponder? I wondered. The names that came to mind were hardly inspiring: Codependency Dale, New Vulnerability, New Sharing.

Yet most Utopian communities—like the one I was standing in—survive only as museums. Perfectionism keeps running aground on the barrier reef of original sin.

A book by Douglas Frank, *Less Than Conquerors*, offers an insightful analysis of the pitfalls of perfectionism. Charles G. Trumbull, a leader in the Victorious Life movement, once said, "It is the privilege of every Christian to live every day of his life without breaking the laws of God in known sin either in thought, word or deed." Such high ideals, observes Frank, paradoxically lead to despair and defeatism. Despite all good efforts, human beings don't achieve a state of sinlessness, and in the end they often blame themselves (a blame encouraged by their leaders: "If it is not working, you must not be believing enough").

Frank points out yet another flaw in perfectionism: too often it disintegrates into pettiness (one of the sharpest criticisms Jesus made of the Pharisees). In an attempt to dilute the delights of the flesh, Charles Finney's Oberlin College banned coffee, tea, pepper, mustard, oil, and vinegar. The experiment didn't last long, as any recent visitor to Oberlin can attest.

I grew up in a climate of severe perfectionism from which I have spent much of life recovering, and I learned firsthand the pettiness of modern fundamentalism. My church debated the morality of bowling alleys ("Don't they serve liquor?") and roller skating ("They hold hands!"), but cared not a whit about human rights in South Africa or civil rights at home in Georgia.

Still, despite a potent inoculation against the abuses of perfectionism, I sometimes feel this nostalgia, even longing, for the quest itself. I read with amazement Thomas Merton's *Ascent to Truth*, which chronicles one man's full-time search for mystical union with God. I burn with shame as I read the Russian classic *The Way of a Pilgrim*, which tells of a peasant who took literally the command "Pray without ceasing" and prayed the Jesus prayer ("Lord Jesus Christ, Son of God, have mercy on me, a sinner") seven thousand times a day.

How can we in the church uphold the ideal of holiness, the proper striving for Life on the Highest Plane, while avoiding the consequences of disillusionment, pettiness, abuse of authority, spiritual pride, and exclusivism?

Or, to ask the opposite question, how can we moderns who emphasize community support (never judgment), vulnerability, and introspection keep from aiming too low? An individualistic society, America is in constant danger of freedom abuse; its churches are in danger of grace abuse.

With these questions in mind, I read through most of the New Testament Epistles, though in a different order than usual. First I read Galatians, with its magnificent charter of Christian liberty and its fiery pronouncements against petty legalism. "It is for freedom that Christ has set us free," Paul declared (5:1). But three paragraphs later he added these words, "But do not use your freedom to indulge the sinful nature; rather, serve one another in love."

Next I turned to James, the "right strawy epistle" that stuck in Martin Luther's throat. I was familiar with James's stern admonitions, but I had not noticed his formula for obtaining holiness. James balanced each prodding to strive harder with the simple advice to depend on God (1:5, 17, 21; 2:24; 4:3, 7; 5:11). "Mercy triumphs over judgment!" he concluded.

I read Ephesians and then 1 Corinthians, Romans and then 1 Timothy, Colossians and then 1 Peter. In every book without exception I found both messages: the high ideals of holiness and also the safety net of grace, a merciful reminder that salvation does not depend on our meeting those ideals. Ephesians pulls the two strands together neatly: "For it is by grace you have been saved, through faith—and this not from yourselves, it is the gift of God—not by works, so that no one can boast. For we are God's workmanship, created in Christ Jesus to do good works, which God prepared in advance for us to do."

I took some comfort in the fact that the church in the first century was already on a seesaw, tilting now toward perfectionistic legalism and now toward raucous antinomianism. James wrote to one extreme; Paul often addressed the other. Each letter had a strong correcting emphasis, but all stressed the dual message of the gospel. The church, in other words, should be both: a people who strive toward holiness and yet relax in grace, a people who judge themselves but not others, a people who depend on God and not themselves.

The seesaw is still lurching back and forth. Some churches tilt one way, some another. My reading of the Epistles left me yearning for a both/and church. I have seen too many either/or congregations.

# Chapter 47

# Having a Bad Hymn Day

For a number of Sunday mornings in a row, I began the day by reading from John Milton's *Paradise Lost*. The language was thrilling, the images ethereal, the themes exalted. Then I proceeded to church, a congregation that sings "praise songs" accompanied by a keyboard and guitars. Without fail, someone requested the children's favorite "Our God Is an Awesome God," which contains the eminently forgettable line, "When He rolls up his sleeves, He ain't just puttin' on the Ritz."

For me, the jarring descent from *Paradise Lost* to "Awesome God" has come to symbolize a major dilemma of aesthetics. How does one appreciate quality without becoming a snob? About some things, I have no snobbery: I wear hand-me-down clothes, stay in budget motels, and drive a boxy, practical car. But I can instantly sniff the difference between coffee brewed by Mr. Coffee and that brewed by Braun. And when it comes to music, I'll always vote for Bach and Mozart over songs built around three major chords and a dull phrase repeated over and over.

How do we encourage Bach while not quenching the spirit of "Kum Ba Yah"? How to appreciate Milton without scorning gospel tracts? Or, to broaden the issue, how do we recognize quality of any type—physical beauty, intelligence, athletic ability—without devaluing those who lack such gifts?

Our world rewards the gifted at the expense of the less gifted. Stand outside a kindergarten playground and watch how children treat playmates who seem clumsy, ugly, or dense. Adults continue the pattern. We pay professional athletes $10 million a year and teachers $40,000. We choose young girls of promising beauty, starve them, pad them, and carve them with a plastic surgeon's knife to transform them into supermodels who will then leave less-endowed females (99.9 percent of the population) with a permanent self-image crisis.

The church has wavered back and forth on the issue of values. Those who followed the *via negativa,* or Negative Way, solved the problem by renouncing all sensual pleasures. They ate diets of bread and water, lashed themselves with whips, and rigorously practiced celibacy. (A neglected side of celibacy: If no one gets married, then no one feels left out, either.) Saint Jerome, an outstanding proponent of this school in the fourth century, had a stunted aesthetic sense but had much time for prayer, worship, and acts of discipline. As I have already mentioned, he sublimated his sexual drive by translating the Hebrew Scriptures, which resulted in the Latin Vulgate Version used for the next millennium.

Saint Augustine, Jerome's contemporary, took a different approach. He had a keen eye for beauty, enjoyed a good Roman feast, and worked to improve his body, mind, and soul. Augustine believed in the essential goodness of created things; the Latin phrase *dona bona*, or "good gifts," appears throughout his *City of God*. The trick, as he saw it, was to maintain a balance between the values of the City of God and the city of this world. "The world is a smiling place," he preached once in a sermon.

Naked stylites who live on poles and ermine-draped bishops who live in palaces point to different ways of resolving the aesthetic dilemma. Today, some churches play Bach on organs more magnificent than Johann himself could have imagined. Others accompany "Awesome God" with a forty-piece orchestra. Still others ban music altogether. I once attended a wedding in which the scratchy strains of Mendelssohn's "Wedding March" came from a turntable positioned well outside the sanctuary; a long extension cord allowed them to circumvent the denominational rule against musical instruments in the church.

If Christian history offers any clue, I doubt anyone will soon come up with a neat formula to resolve these matters. But I do believe that Christianity, and only Christianity, has three essential contributions to make:

1. Good things are a gift, not a possession. Augustine got it right with his phrase *dona bona*. We are creatures who have been loaned talent, beauty, and intelligence by a Creator who intended us to use them well. Created things still retain glimmers of essential goodness, hints of a divine origin. G. K. Chesterton draws the analogy of Robinson Crusoe on a rock island tenderly collecting the few comforts he could snatch from the sea, sacred relics of the sinking ship.

2. In this fallen world, good things are remnants that have been spoiled. The human Fall changed everything, and now every good thing presents an implicit risk as well and contains within it the potential for exploitation and

abuse. Think of sex, of food, of our planet's grand resources. Power, beauty, and brilliance are all good things, qualities possessed by our Creator, but human history amply demonstrates what can happen to these in the hands of human beings who have tasted of the tree of the knowledge of good and evil.

3. Even spoiled things can be made good. I have observed in art museums that saints are rather ugly, portrayed with gaunt faces, aquiline noses, and scraggly hair. I do not know whether they chose a path that led them to sainthood because of social ostracism (just as many researcher scientists—and writers, for that matter—are bookish introverts), or whether their appearance suffered as the demands of sainthood took a physical toll. Regardless, saints by definition bear out a lasting truth of the Sermon on the Mount: God judges by different standards, and the poor and lowly, who suffer disadvantage in the city of man, have a real advantage in the City of God. Consider the heroes of Jesus' stories: the shabby beggar Lazarus, a widow with two pennies to her name, a despicable tax collector. Consider the end of Jesus' own story: from a brutal execution came the salvation of the world.

I take comfort in the fact that Christianity, while honoring God's good gifts, still finds an esteemed place for those who lack them. In the City of God, a paralyzed Joni Eareckson leaps and dances with Olympian grace. And as for my original quandary about music in church, I am trying to learn a lesson from C. S. Lewis, who wrote this about his (Anglican!) church:

I disliked very much their hymns, which I considered to be fifth-rate poems set to sixth-rate music. But as I went on I saw the great merit of it. . . . I realized that the hymns (which were just sixth-rate music) were, nevertheless, being sung with devotion and benefit by an old saint in elastic-side boots in the opposite pew, and then you realize that you aren't fit to clean those boots. It gets you out of your solitary conceit.

Chapter 48

# Dear Mr. Chicken:
# Please Send Money

For a period of one month, I tossed every fund-raising appeal from the day's mail into a large box. Then I emptied and read the contents of that box: sixty-two separate appeals, weighing a total of 3.5 pounds. It terrified me. Without my immediate help, the world may come crashing down sometime next week.

First I perused the political appeals, an assortment of phony surveys and fake telegrams. The political fortunes of the Religious Right alarmed liberal politicians, whereas conservatives seemed preoccupied with the social agenda of the Democratic Party.

Next came a series of appeals from environmental causes, including my favorite, Friends of the Musk Ox. Unless I act, miners and loggers will despoil Alaska's remaining wilderness, zebra mussels will swallow Lake Michigan, and old-growth forests will fall to the chain saws. (How many young-growth forests die to provide paper for the fund-raising packets designed to save old-growth forests?)

The rest of the stack of mail, more than two-thirds of the total, came from religious groups. Some years ago I gave money to an organization aiding Soviet dissidents, who happened to be Jewish. Now Simon Wiesenthal is one of my most faithful correspondents, and I also receive appeals from obscure Jewish organizations. Consider this letter from Judge Wapner, formerly presider over *People's Court*, now writing on behalf of the National Institute for Jewish Hospice: "Have you ever walked past a poor old soul lying on a gurney in a cold hospital corridor? . . . Her pallid cheeks are sunken, her hair white and lifeless, her bones almost without flesh. . . ."

I got appeals from Catholic orders, too. The Passionist Monastery assured me that for a minimum ten-dollar contribution, I can have twelve loved ones in Purgatory remembered in a special Mass on All Souls' Day. Or I could send my money to Servants of the Paraclete to assist with rehabilitation of fallen priests and brothers—a growth industry, apparently.

By far the majority of the stack, however, bore the return addresses of evangelical organizations. What struck me first is how closely they resembled the appeals from everybody else: the same fake "Expressgrams" with the red URGENT! headlines, the same P.S.'s underlined in blue ink, the same "challenge grants" that require me to act within ten days if I want my donation to double in value. These folks must all attend the same seminars.

An editor at *Time* magazine once figured out that one complete direct mail package, including postage and list rental, costs about twenty-six cents. The cost increases if the letter is personalized, "Dear Mr. Yancey." This personalization, by the way, is an inexact science. My neighbor, Popeye's Chicken, gets letters addressed "Dear Mr. Chicken." The Assembly of God headquarters once got a letter with the greeting "Dear Ms. God."

Many people don't know that when an organization rents lists to prospect for new donors, perhaps only one in one hundred people will respond. (This practice, called "cold prospecting," is not to be confused with Arctic mining activities.) Thus it may cost the organization twenty-six dollars to extract your first twenty-five-dollar contribution. The *Time* editor perniciously sent five-dollar donations to organizations he opposed, such as the NRA, just to watch them spend many times that amount trying to squeeze more dollars out of him.

I oppose that editor's clever but wasteful suggestion, and I am trying hard not to be cynical about this whole business of fund-raising. After all, I have written fund-raising letters myself, and I sympathize with an organization's need to communicate to donors. Indeed, the reason I receive so many fund-raising letters is that I support worthwhile organizations and respond to their appeals.

But when is enough enough? After reading sixty-two appeal letters in a row, I was impressed mainly by all the gimmicks employed. A group soliciting money for Bibles for Russia had a catchy red "Approved: Government of Russia" stamp on the envelope. One Christian television station promised me a miracle if I would give a multiple of seven: $7.77, $77.77, or $777.77; the largest amount also earns me a framed original page from a 1564 Bible. A friend of mine wrote this station back, suggesting that they send him the contribution and let God reward them instead of him with the large multiple of blessings they had promised.

I had accumulated a large collection of VHS tapes highlighting the work of various missions before I finally broke down and bought a VCR. To my chagrin, most of them were only ten minutes long and could not be recycled or used for taping. Now I'm accumulating a stack of DVDs in anticipation of my next slow-motion advancement into technology.

One organization graciously sent me a check for fifteen hundred dollars. Alas, I discovered that the check was made out not to me, but to the organization that had sent it, as a crafty way of underscoring a challenge grant. "This facsimile check is valid only if accompanied by a check of equal or greater amount from Mr. & Mrs. Philip D. Yancey."

One mission boasts about its practice of never asking for money directly. It's funny, though, how many urgent "prayer requests" I get from them, asking me to pray for, say, the desperately needed total of sixteen thousand dollars by March 1. I have the utmost respect for OMF, successor to the old China Inland Mission, which actually does follow a rigorous policy of never asking for funds. It took me several weeks to track down their address, and I've never gotten an appeal from them since!

Fund-raising requests tend to follow current events, and it appears that the Middle East and Africa have now replaced Eastern Europe as the crisis of choice. Whereas a few years ago I was being asked to help distribute Bibles in Red Square and save AIDS children in Romania, now I am asked to support refugees in Sudan and sponsor translation of a children's Bible storybook into Arabic ("Exact locations cannot be revealed because disclosure may be life-threatening").

A letter from the American Leprosy Mission evoked much sympathy, but perhaps not for the reasons its senders intended: I felt sad for an organization that must faithfully do battle against such an old-fashioned problem. Although there are 12 million persons with leprosy in the world, the disease never makes the "hot list" in anyone's catalog of emergencies. Which brings up another problem. Any foreign aid organization will tell you that sewers and clean water supplies have far more impact on health than a crash program of doctors and medical supplies—but try to raise money for a sewer system!

In order to get some perspective on this issue, I turned to 2 Corinthians 8–9 and read the longest fund-raising appeal in the

Bible. It is a masterpiece of pressure diplomacy. The apostle Paul heaps praise on the generous Macedonians in hopes of stirring the competitive instincts of his target audience, the Corinthians. He holds up the ultimate example of Jesus: "though he was rich, yet for your sakes he became poor." He lauds the Corinthians in advance for their anticipated gift.

Yet here is a very strange thing. I search these chapters in vain for any clue as to what the Corinthians are being asked to give *for*. Paul directs attention not to the Jews threatened by famine near Jerusalem (Romans 15:25), but to the comfortable donors themselves. He spotlights not the needy recipients (starving Jewish children in the desert), but rather the donors (spiritually enriched believers in Corinth).

In Paul's passage, the only urgent pleading comes from other donors who "urgently pleaded with us for the privilege of sharing in this service to the saints." What makes giving a privilege? Paul extols giving as a spiritual discipline that demonstrates the sincerity of Christian love, follows in the footsteps of Christ, and honors the Lord himself. As a final bonus, giving offers an outstanding witness to the watching world: ". . . men will praise God for the obedience . . . and for your generosity."

God loves a cheerful giver, not a reluctant one, Paul declares in this passage. No wonder. Once we understand giving's value *to ourselves*, not to the recipients, we can't help sneaking a grin. Giving, like love, never diminishes us, for blessings redound upon the happy donor. In Paul's words, giving helps to "enlarge the harvest of your righteousness."

After reading Paul's letter, I went back through all sixty-two appeals for my funds. Not a single one took the high road of focusing on my need as a Christian to honor and obey God by fulfilling his command. The benefits they mentioned were much more temporal: a photo calendar, my name in an honor roll of contributors, a listing in the annual report, a free book worth $14.95.

So who's right, the fund-raising experts who have concluded that American Christians are too self-interested to respond to any such high-minded appeals, or the apostle Paul, who broke every fund-raising rule in the book? If only we had the donor records from Corinth. . . .

# Chapter 49

# God's Colonizers

*American Sermons*, a 939-page anthology in the prestigious Library of America series, includes sermons from Unitarians, Jews, and a Mormon. Yet forty-five of the fifty-three preachers are avowed Christians, with conservatives generously represented by such names as D. L. Moody, J. Gresham Machen, Billy Sunday, Aimée Semple McPherson, and R. A. Torrey as well as a strong contingent of Puritans.

I cannot fathom how a compiler would omit George Whitefield, Charles Finney, and Billy Graham—could a history of baseball overlook Ty Cobb, Babe Ruth, and Barry Bonds?—but in general the editor, Michael Warner, did an admirable service for anyone interested in American preaching. (Warner, who grew up Pentecostal, graduated from Oral Roberts University, came out of the closet as gay, and then departed from the faith, becoming, in his own words, "a queer atheist intellectual.")

Modern preachers owe a great debt to the Puritans, who elevated the sermon to a place of honor. The Anglican Church had downgraded sermons to quarterly events, and Catholics had likewise deemphasized the homily. English Puritans risked arrest by meeting illicitly to hear sermons, and those who emigrated to America made the most of their freedom. Increase Mather, for example, spent sixteen hours a day in his study and recited his hourlong sermons from memory.

More than a century later, slave preachers were fashioning a new style of preaching, based not on linear reasoning but rather on soaring figures of speech. "Like a chained eagle my soul rises toward her native heben, but she can only fly just so high," cried Brother Carper. "But de fetters ob flesh shall fall off soon. . . ."

Southern revivalism confronted white audiences with a strong emotional appeal. Sam P. Jones, a former drunk, stood atop an old piano box and railed against the dangers of meanness, whiskey, and Democrats to a crowd of twelve thousand people. Billy Sunday, a professional baseball player and son of a Union Army soldier, declared that "there has never been a time when it is harder to live a consistent Christian life than now." He pronounced the allurements of sin more dangerous in his day than at any time since Adam and Eve.

Tellingly, representative sermons from the twentieth century are half the length of those in prior centuries, far more genteel, and as likely to be psychological as theological in their thrust.

Taken together, the sermons give a capsule history of the United States. Famous preachers of modern times, especially those who speak on radio and television, emphasize success and "health and wealth." Such an emphasis apparently never occurred to the tiny knot of Puritan settlers, only half of whom survived their first winter in a place they dubbed "New England." Even so, early immigrants envisioned themselves entering the Promised

Land of possibility and freedom. The later legions of slaves brought from Africa in chains found it easier to identify with the Israelites in bondage in Egypt.

Every era has its preferred sins. Today we hear sermons about the evils of abortion and homosexuality. Earlier congregations heard about witchcraft, demon rum, rampant capitalism, and foreign entanglements. During Civil War days, preachers in both North and South quoted the Bible to justify their region's convictions.

John Winthrop preached his famous "Citty upon a Hill" sermon aboard a ship bringing settlers to America. "The eies of all people are uppon us," he said, and if America failed to meet its ideals, "wee shall be made a story and a by-word throughout the world." Almost two centuries later, the former slave Absalom Jones preached a powerful Thanksgiving sermon honoring Congress for abolishing the African slave trade. Little did he know that another fifty-five years would pass before slaves already in America would receive their freedom.

Fast forward another century, and Martin Luther King Jr. was still repeating the simple refrain, "We want to be free." King is one of five individuals who merits two sermons in this anthology: the "I've been to the mountaintop" sermon preached on the eve of his assassination, and "Transformed Nonconformist," which explores the Christian's citizenship in two worlds.

"Who is it that is supposed to articulate the longings and aspirations of the people more than the preacher?" King asked. Quoting Philippians, King urged believers to establish a "colony of heaven" here on earth—not to be content as "thermometers that record or register the temperature of majority opinion," rather to become "thermostats, that transform and regulate the temperature of society."

A haunting question from King's six-year-old daughter echoes across time for all who try to colonize Heaven in an imperfect world: "Daddy, why do you have to go to jail so much?" No doubt the Puritans in England heard similar questions from their own children before sailing off to establish a City upon a Hill, a city whose ideals modern preachers are still urging us to realize.

# About the Author

Philip Yancey is the author of twenty books with a total of more than 7 million copies in print. They include *Soul Survivor*, *Where Is God When It Hurts?*, *What's So Amazing About Grace?*, and most recently, *Rumors of Another World*. He lives in Colorado with his wife, Janet.